budgetbooks

MOVIE SONGS

ISBN 0-634-08064-4

7777 W. BLUEMOUND RD. P.O. BOX 13819 MILWAUKEE, WI 53213

Visit Hal Leonard Online at
www.halleonard.com

CONTENTS

ALL FOR LOVE
from Walt Disney Pictures' THE THREE MUSKETEERS

Words and Music by BRYAN ADAMS,
ROBERT JOHN "MUTT" LANGE and MICHAEL KAMEN

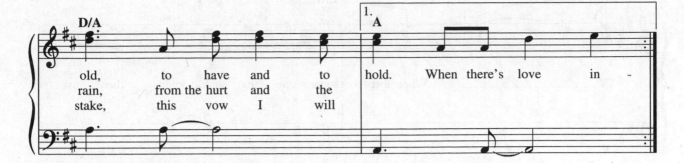

old, to have and to hold. When there's love in -
rain, from the hurt and to the
stake, this vow I will

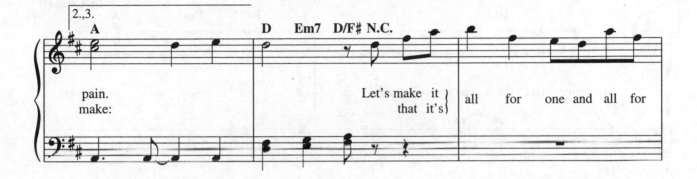

pain.
make: Let's make it all for one and all for
that it's

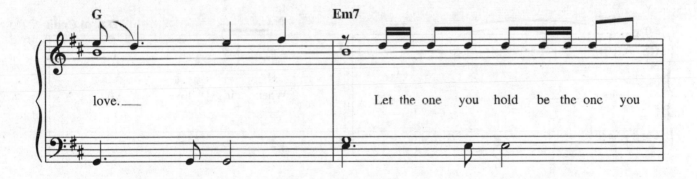

love.___ Let the one you hold be the one you

want, the one you need, 'cause when it's all for one it's one for

6

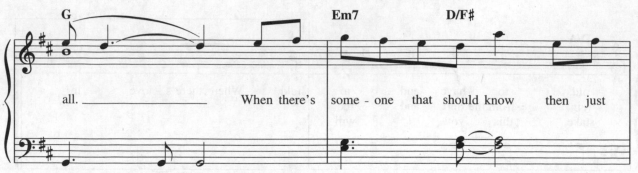

all. _____ When there's some-one that should know then just

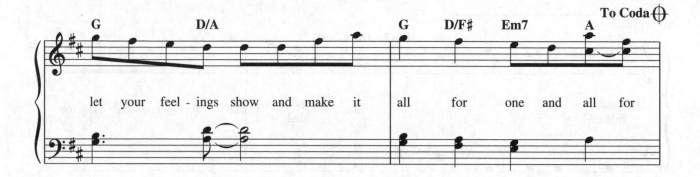

let your feel-ings show and make it all for one and all for

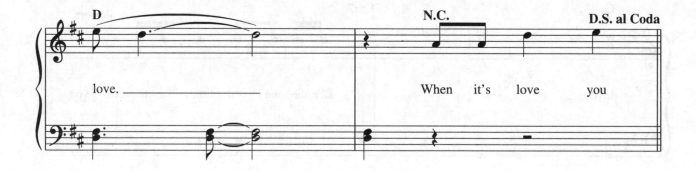

love. _____ When it's love you

CODA

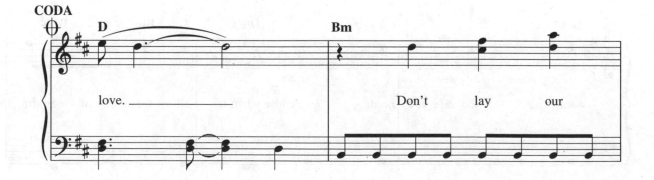

love. _____ Don't lay our

love to rest _ 'cause we could stand up to the test. We got ev - 'ry - thing _ and

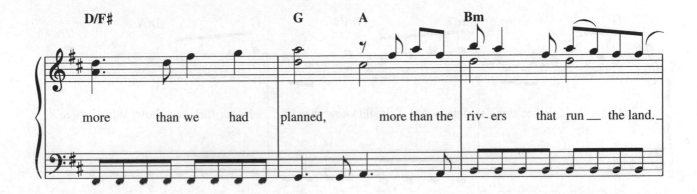

more than we had planned, more than the riv - ers that run _ the land. _

_ We've got it all _ in our hands. Now it's

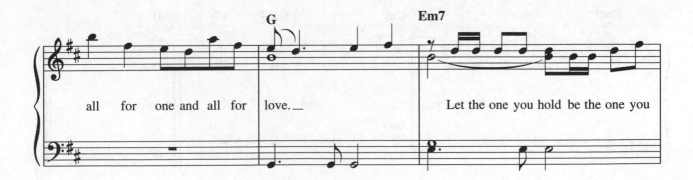

all for one and all for love. _ Let the one you hold be the one you

want, the one you need, 'cause when it's all for one it's one for

all. _____ When there's some-one that should know then just let your feel-ings show. When there's

some - one that you want, when there's some - one that you need, let's make it

all, all for one _____ and all for love.

ALMOST PARADISE
Love Theme from the Paramount Motion Picture FOOTLOOSE

Words by DEAN PITCHFORD
Music by ERIC CARMEN

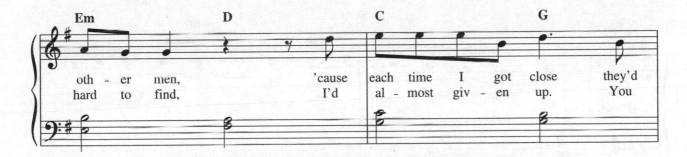

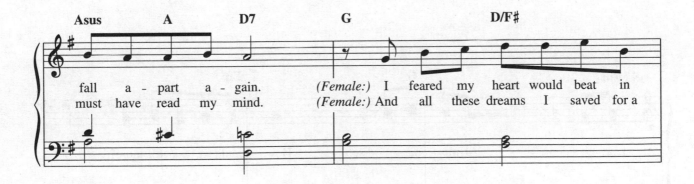

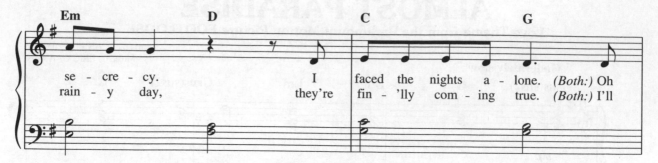

se - cre - cy. / rain - y day, ... I / they're ... faced the nights a - lone. *(Both:)* Oh / fin - 'lly com - ing true. *(Both:)* I'll

how could I have known / share them all with you, ... that / 'cause all my life I on - ly need - ed / now we hold the fu - ture in our

you? / hands. ... Oh, ____ al - most par - a - dise, _____ We're knock-in' on

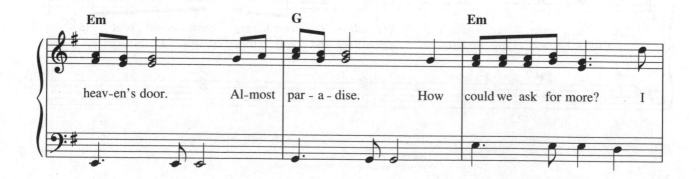

heav - en's door. Al-most par - a - dise. How could we ask for more? I

To Coda ⊕

swear that I can see for - ev - er in your __ eyes. Par - a - dise.

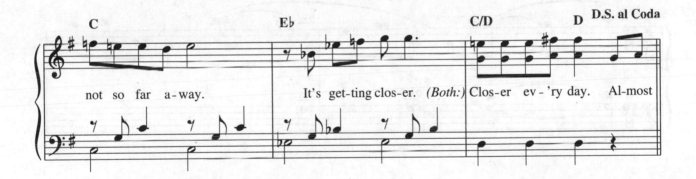

(Male:)
And in your arms, sal - va-tion's

D.S. al Coda

not so far a - way. It's get-ting clos-er. *(Both:)* Clos-er ev-'ry day. Al-most

CODA

rit. e dim. Par - a - dise. *p*

THEME FROM ANGELA'S ASHES

Paramount Pictures and Universal Pictures International Present ANGELA'S ASHES

Music by JOHN WILLIAMS

Slow, gently flowing

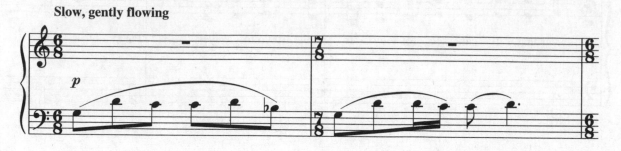

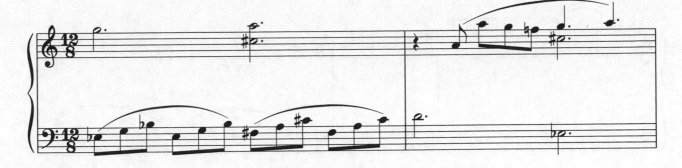

Reflectively

With motion

Moderately

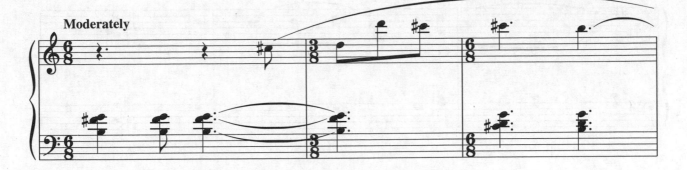

Original tempo

BABY ELEPHANT WALK

from the Paramount Picture HATARI!

By HENRY MANCINI

22

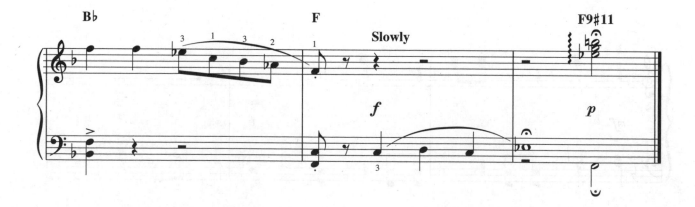

BLESS THE BEASTS AND CHILDREN

from BLESS THE BEASTS AND CHILDREN

Words and Music by BARRY DeVORZON
and PERRY BOTKIN, JR.

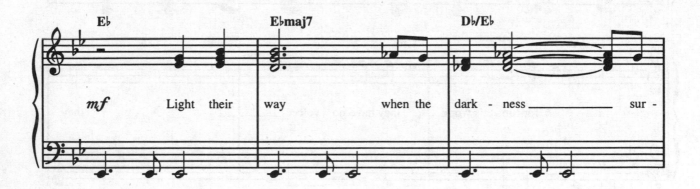

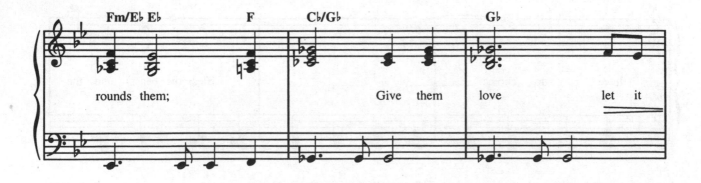

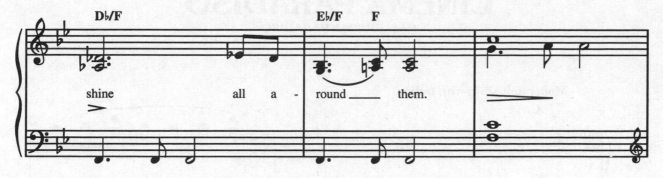

shine   all a - round _____ them.

mp Bless the beasts and the chil - dren;   Give them shel - ter

from   a   storm; _____   Keep   them safe; _____

_____   Keep   them warm.
rit.

CINEMA PARADISO

from CINEMA PARADISO

Music by ENNIO MORRICONE

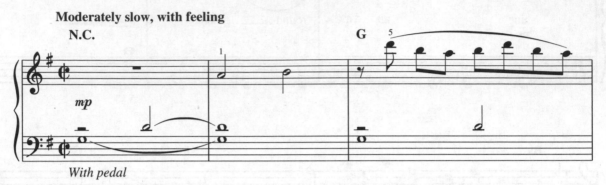

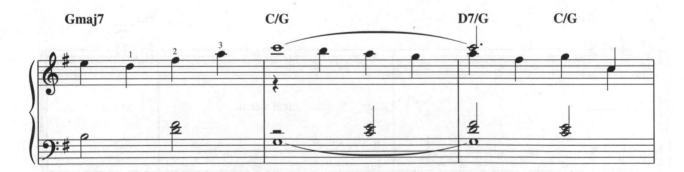

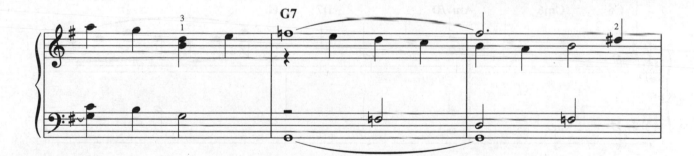

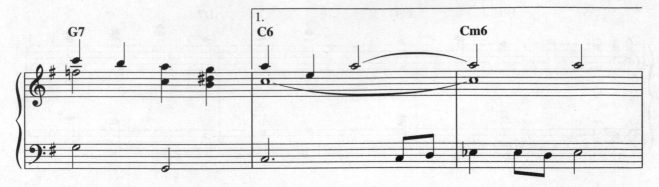

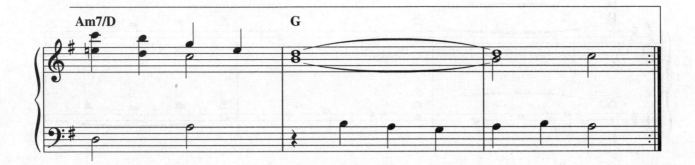

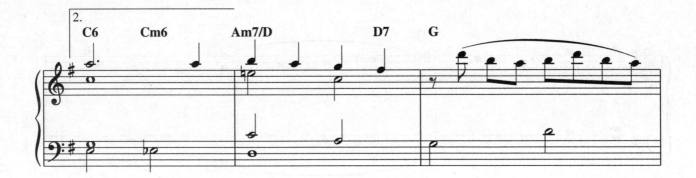

COME WHAT MAY

from the Motion Picture MOULIN ROUGE

Words and Music by
DAVID BAERWALD

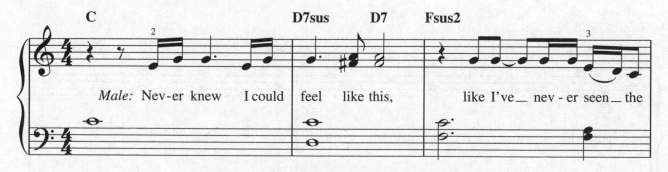

Male: Nev-er knew I could feel like this, like I've_ nev-er seen_ the

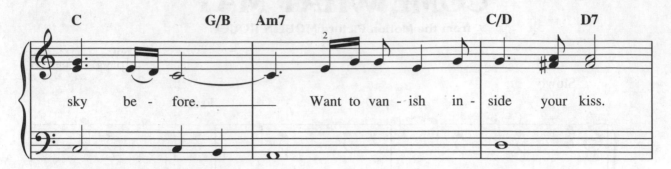

sky be - fore._____ Want to van - ish in - side your kiss.

Ev - 'ry day___ I love___ you more and___ more.

Lis - ten to my heart. Can you hear it sing and

tell - ing me to give___ you ev - 'ry - thing?

Sea - sons may change, win - ter to spring, but I

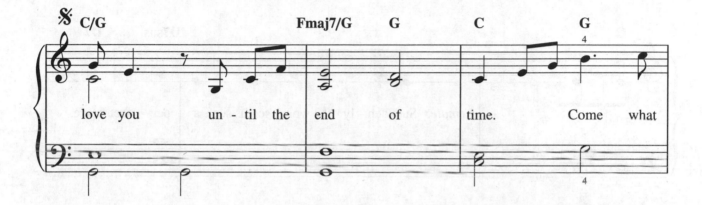

love you un - til the end of time. Come what

may, come what

may, I will

32

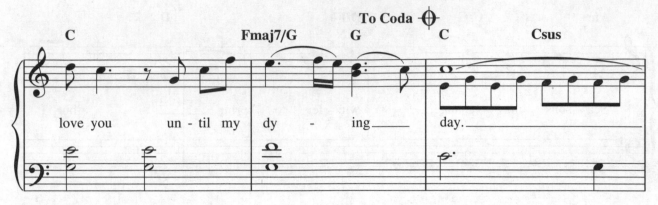

love you   un - til my   dy - ing____   day.____

Female: Sud - den - ly the world seems such a   per - fect place.

Sud - den - ly it moves with   such__ a   per - fect__ grace.____

Both: Sud - den - ly my life does - n't   seem_____ such a   waste.__

Fsus2 / C

Female: It all re - volves__ a - round__ you. *Both:* And there's no

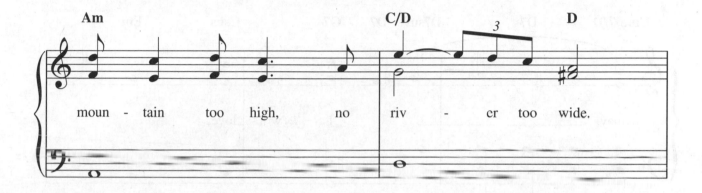

Am / C/D / D

moun - tain too high, no riv - er too wide.

Gsus / G / Csus / C / G/B

Sing out__ this song, and I'll be there__ by your side.

Am / Am/G / D/F♯ / D / D.S. al Coda

Storm clouds may gath - er and stars__ may col - lide,__ *Male:* but I

34

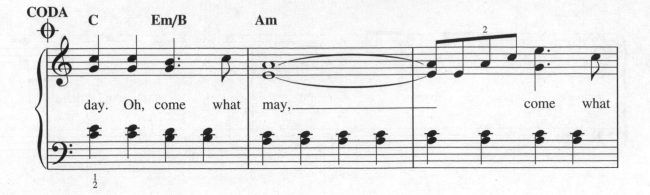

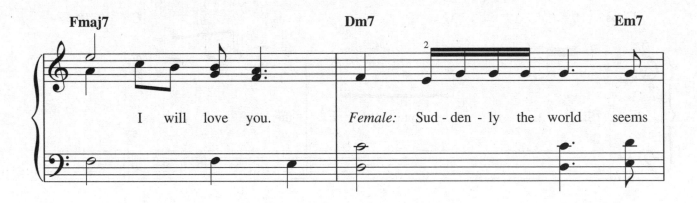

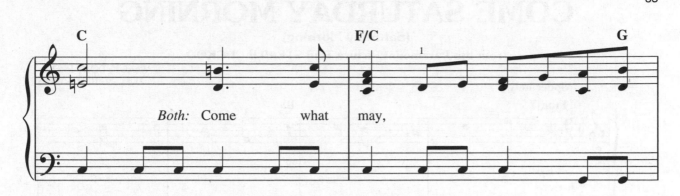

Both: Come what may,

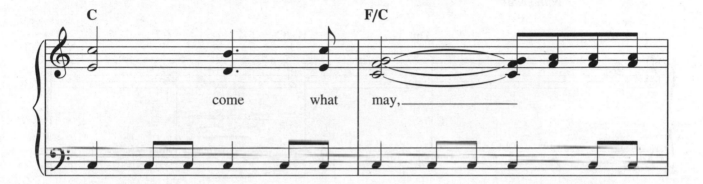

come what may,_____

I will love you_____ un - til my

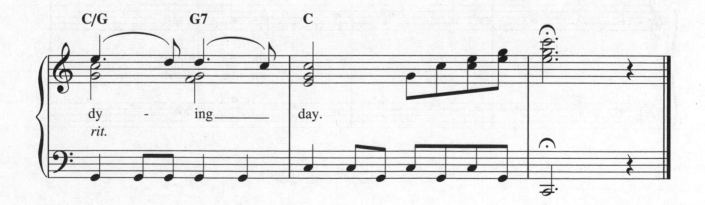

dy - ing_____ day.
rit.

COME SATURDAY MORNING
(Saturday Morning)
from the Paramount Picture THE STERILE CUCKOO

Words by DORY PREVIN
Music by FRED KARLIN

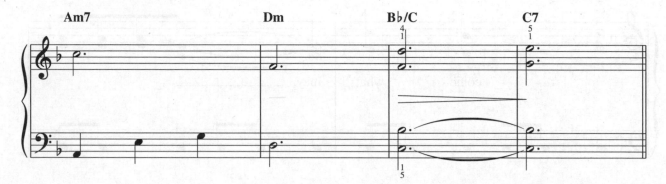

Come Sat - ur - day morn - ing
Come Sat - ur - day morn - ing

I'm go - ing a - way with my friend;
I'm go - ing a - way with my friend;

We'll Sat - ur - day spend till the end of the
We'll Sat - ur - day laugh more than half of the

day. _____
day. _____

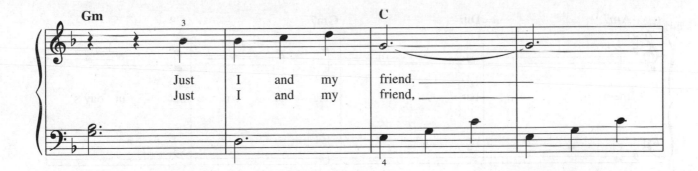

Just I and my friend. _____
Just I and my friend, _____

We'll trav - el for miles in our Sat - ur - day
dressed up in our rings and our Sat - ur - day

38

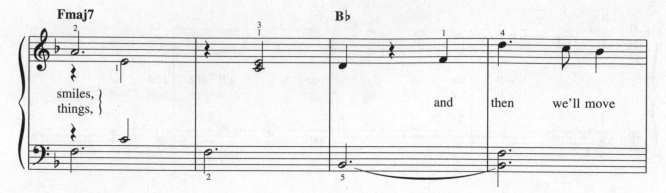

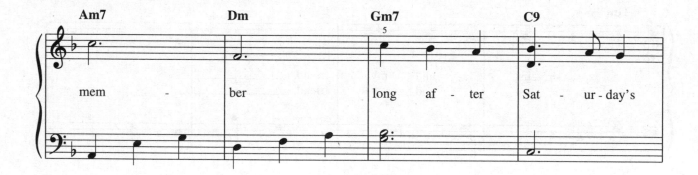

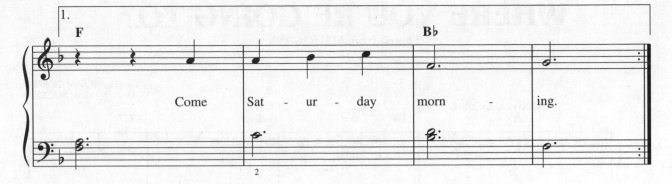

1.

Come Sat - ur - day morn - - ing.

2.

Come Sat - ur - day morn - - ing.

Come Sat - ur - day morn - - ing.

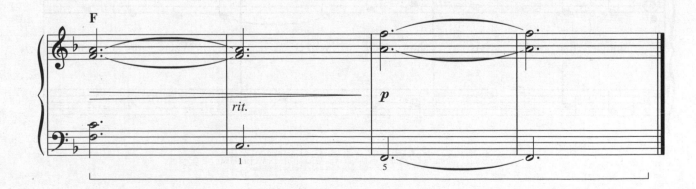

rit.   p

Do You Know Where You're Going To?

Theme from MAHOGANY

Words by GERRY GOFFIN
Music by MIKE MASSER

Do you know where you're go - ing to? Do you like the

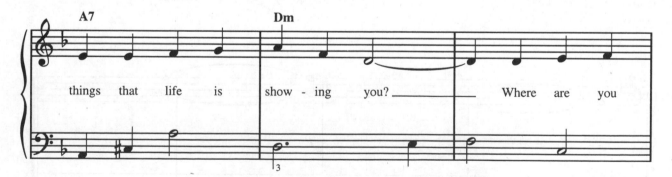

things that life is show - ing you? Where are you

42

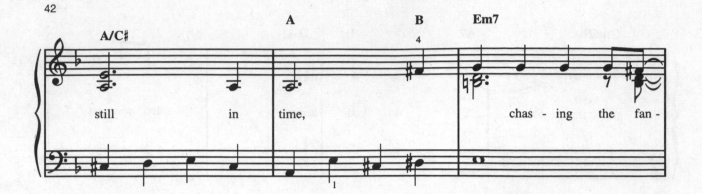

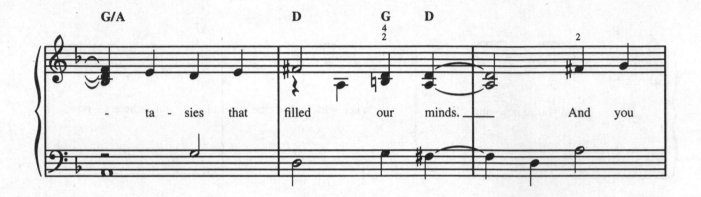

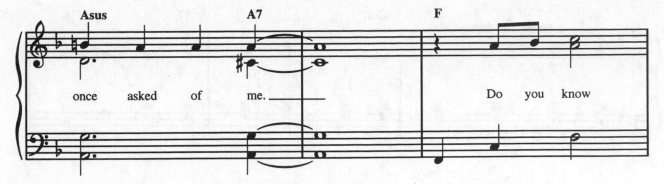

once asked of me. ___ Do you know

where you're go - ing to? Do you like the things that life is

show - ing you? ___ Where are you go - ing to, ___

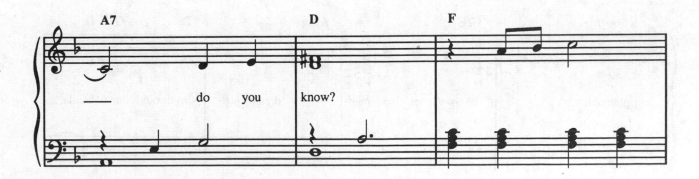

___ do you know?

44

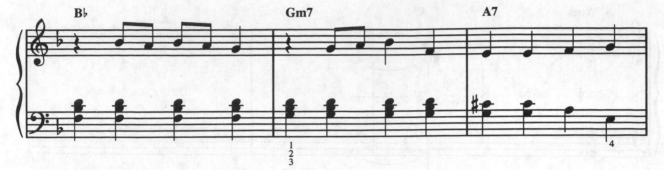

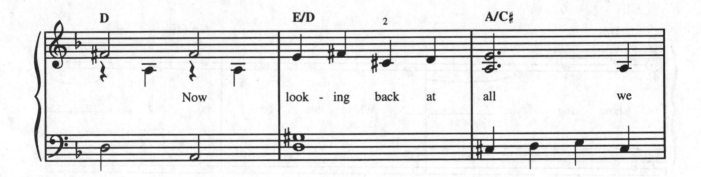

Now look-ing back at all we

planned, we let so man- - y dreams just slip through our hands. _

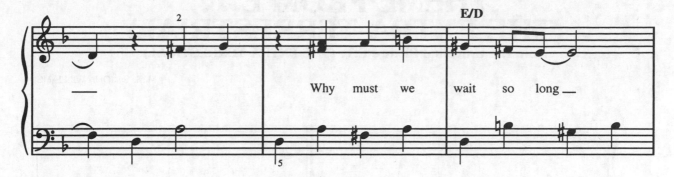

Why must we wait so long ___

be - fore we see   how sad the an -

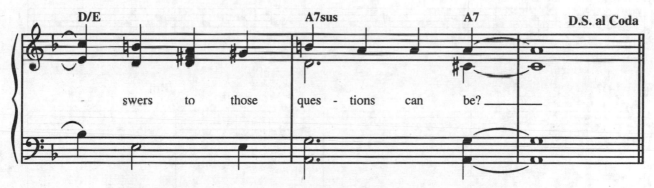

swers to those ques - tions can be? ___

know?

THEME FROM E.T.
(THE EXTRA-TERRESTRIAL)

from the Universal Picture E.T. (THE EXTRA-TERRESTRIAL)

Music by JOHN WILLIAMS

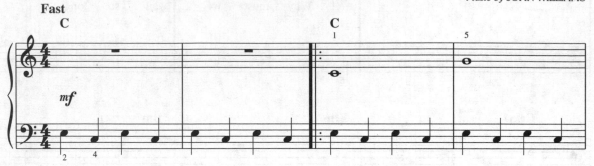

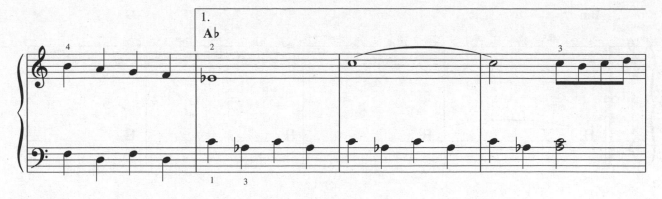

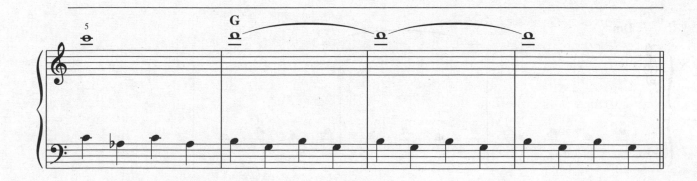

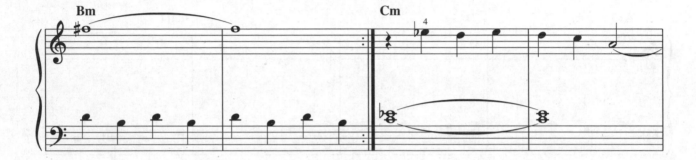

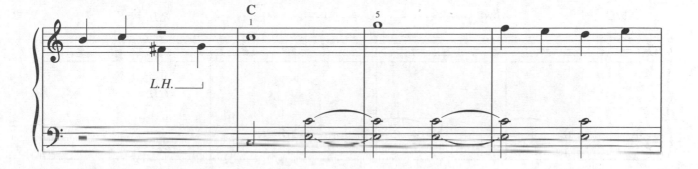

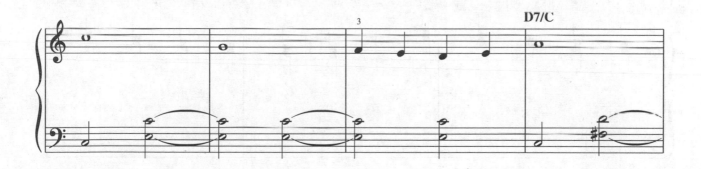

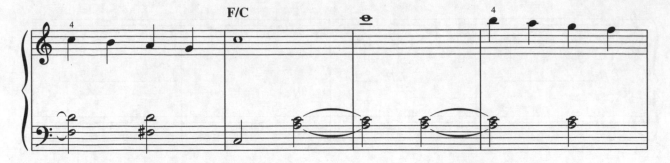

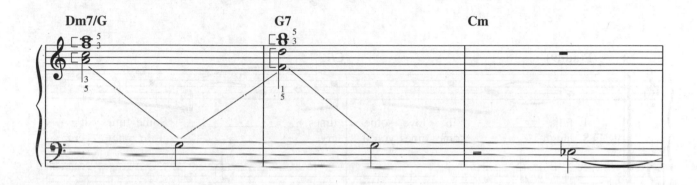

Dm7/G G7 Cm

C

EXHALE
(Shoop Shoop)
from the Original Soundtrack Album WAITING TO EXHALE

Words and Music by
BABYFACE

Easy R&B Ballad

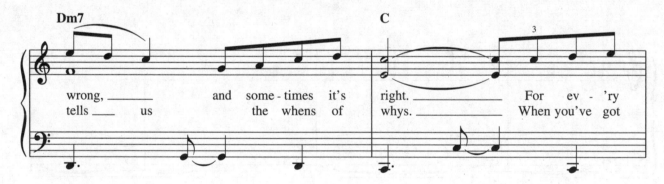

53

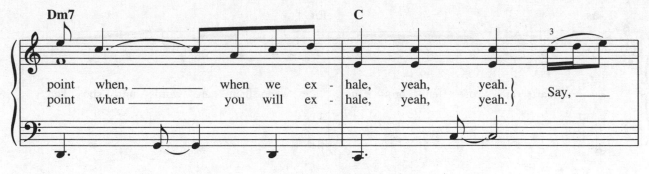

point when, _____ when we ex - hale, yeah, yeah.
point when _____ you will ex - hale, yeah, yeah.

Say, _____

shoop shoop shoop shoo be doo. Shoop shoop shoo be doo. Shoop shoop shoo be

doo. Shoop shoop shoo be doo. Shoop shoop shoo be doo. Shoop shoop shoo be

doo. Shoop shoop shoo be doo. _____ Some-times you'll doo.

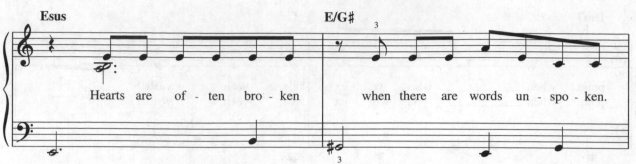

Hearts are of-ten bro-ken when there are words un-spo-ken.

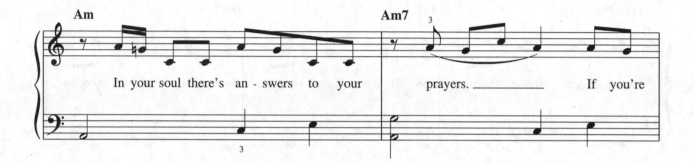

In your soul there's an-swers to your prayers. _____ If you're

search-ing for a place you know, a fa-mil-iar face, some-where to go, you should

look in-side your soul; __ you're half-way there. _____ Some-times you'll   doo.

THE EXODUS SONG

from EXODUS

Words by PAT BOONE
Music by ERNEST GOLD

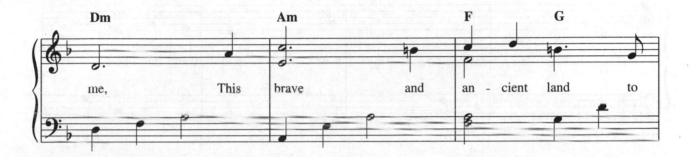

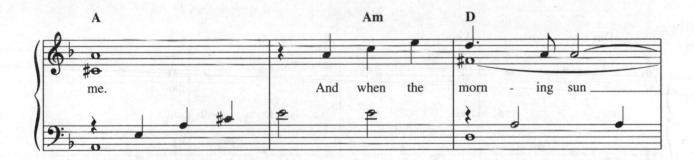

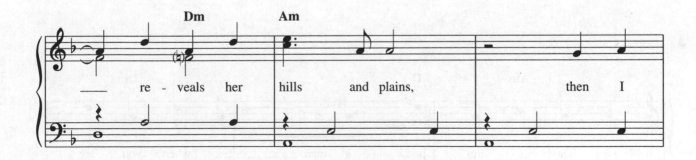

THE EXODUS SONG

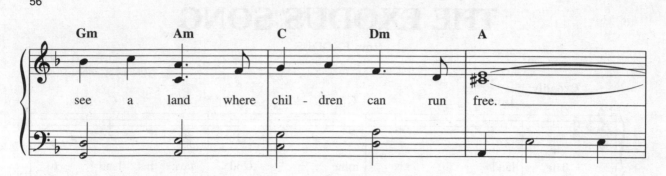

see a land where chil - dren can run free.

So take my hand and walk this land with

me, And walk this love - ly land with me.

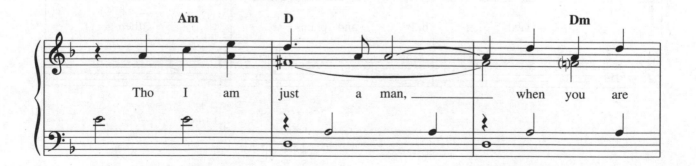

Tho I am just a man, when you are

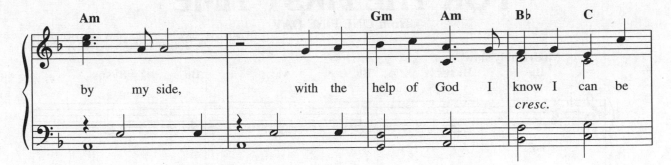

by my side, with the help of God I know I can be

cresc.

strong. To make this land our home,

_f_

If

I must fight, I'll fight to make this land our own.

Un-

_ff_

til I die this land is mine!

rit.

_8vb_

FOR THE FIRST TIME

from ONE FINE DAY

Words and Music by JAMES NEWTON HOWARD
JUD FRIEDMAN and ALLAN RICH

mine?
Now I won-der how I could have been so

be?
All a- long this love was right in front of

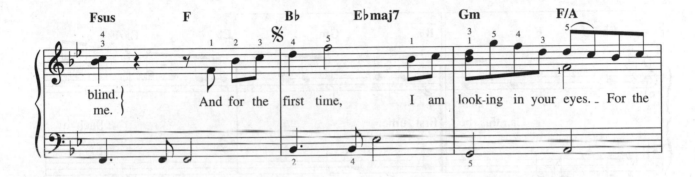

blind.
me.

And for the first time, I am look-ing in your eyes._ For the

first time I'm___ see-ing who you are.___ I can't be -

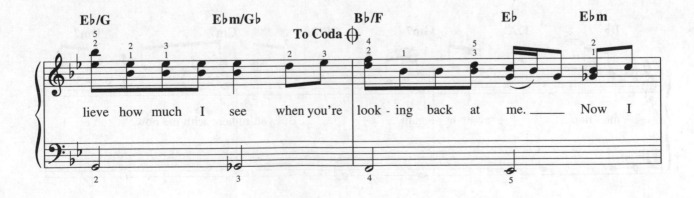

lieve how much I see when you're look-ing back at me.___ Now I

60

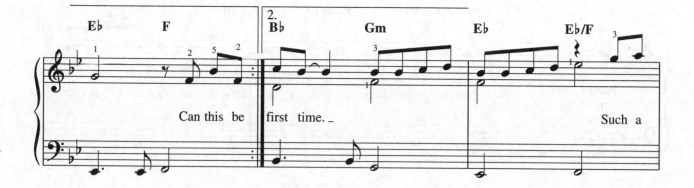

THE FRIENDSHIP THEME

from Touchstone Pictures' BEACHES

Music by GEORGES DELERUE

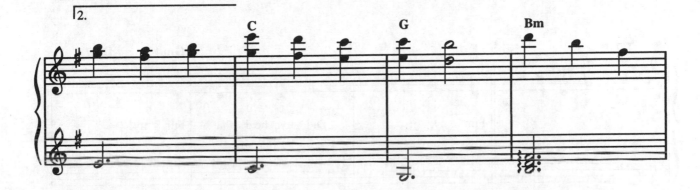

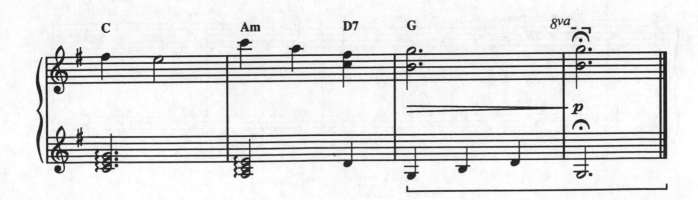

FUNNY GIRL

from FUNNY GIRL

Words by BOB MERRILL
Music by JULE STYNE

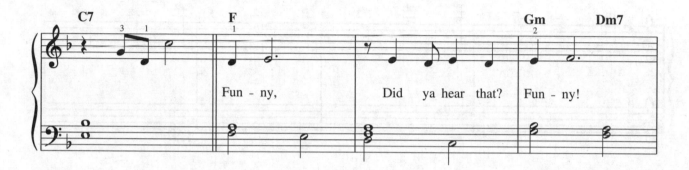

Fun - ny, Did ya hear that? Fun - ny!

Yes, the guy said: "Hon - ey, you're a fun - ny girl!"____

____ That's me, ____ I just keep them in stitch - es, Dou - bled in half.

And tho' I may be all wrong for the guy, __ I'm

good   for a laugh. ___   I   guess __ it's not   fun - ny,

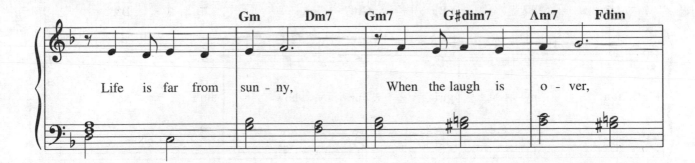

Life   is far from   sun - ny,   When the laugh is   o - ver,

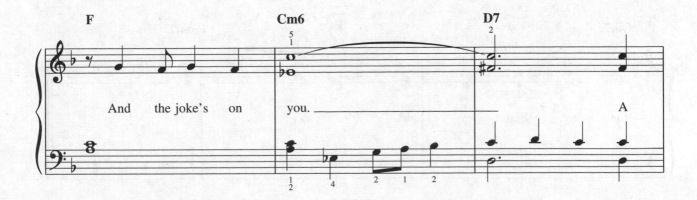

And   the joke's on   you. _____   A

girl ought to have a sense of hu - mor, That's one thing you real - ly need for

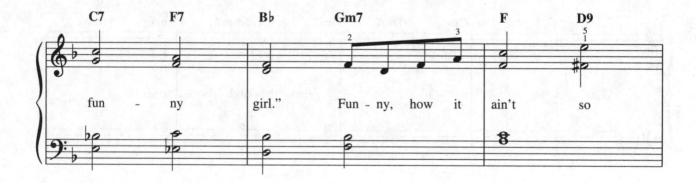

sure When you're a fun - ny girl, The fel - low said, "A

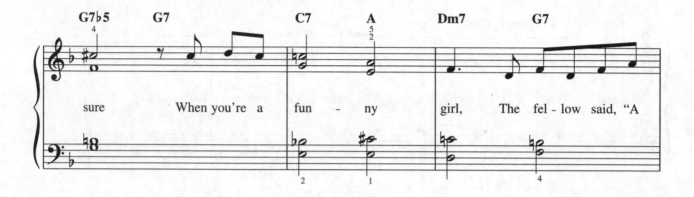

fun - ny girl." Fun - ny, how it ain't so

fun - ny, Fun - ny girl. *rit.*

GIRL TALK
from the Paramount Picture HARLOW

Words by BOBBY TROUP
Music by NEAL HEFTI

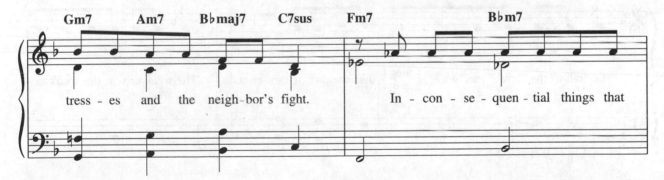

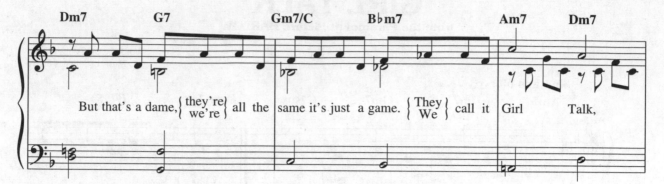

But that's a dame, {they're / we're} all the same it's just a game. {They / We} call it Girl Talk,

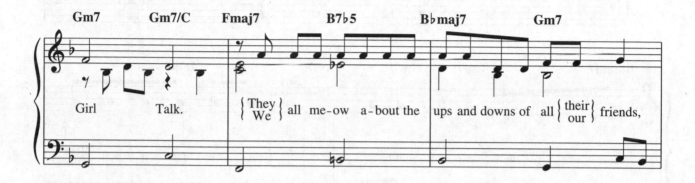

Girl Talk. {They / We} all me-ow a-bout the ups and downs of all {their / our} friends,

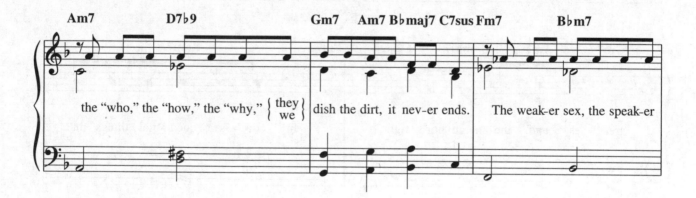

the "who," the "how," the "why," {they / we} dish the dirt, it nev-er ends. The weak-er sex, the speak-er

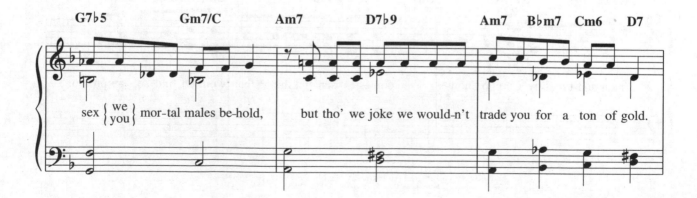

sex {we / you} mor-tal males be-hold, but tho' we joke we would-n't trade you for a ton of gold.

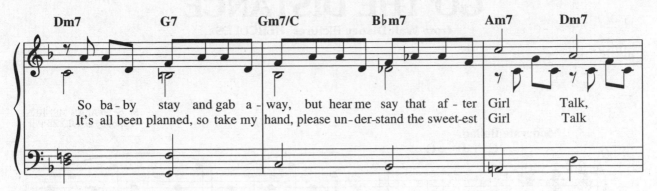

So ba - by stay and gab a - way, but hear me say that af - ter Girl Talk,
It's all been planned, so take my hand, please un - der - stand the sweet - est Girl Talk

talk to me.
talks of,

Girl Talk talks of, Girl Talk

talks of you, of you.

GO THE DISTANCE

from Walt Disney Pictures' HERCULES

Music by ALAN MENKEN
Lyrics by DAVID ZIPPEL

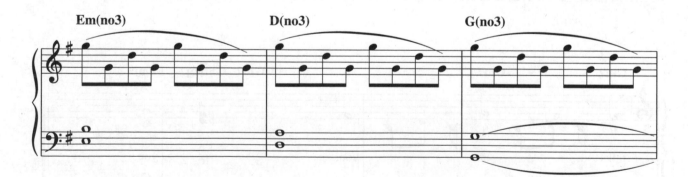

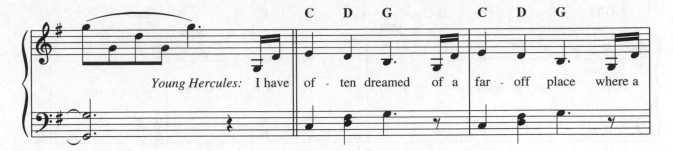

Young Hercules: I have of-ten dreamed of a far-off place where a

great warm wel-come will be wait - ing for me. Where the crowds will cheer when they

see my face, and a voice keeps say-ing this is where I'm meant to be. _____ I will

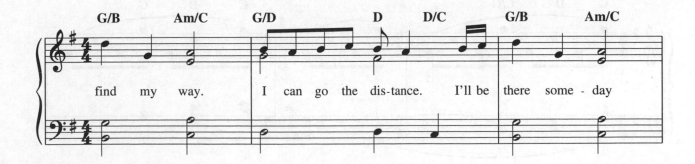

find my way. I can go the dis-tance. I'll be there some - day

if I can be strong. I know ev - 'ry mile will be worth my

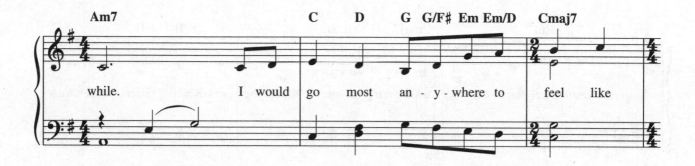

while. I would go most an - y - where to feel like

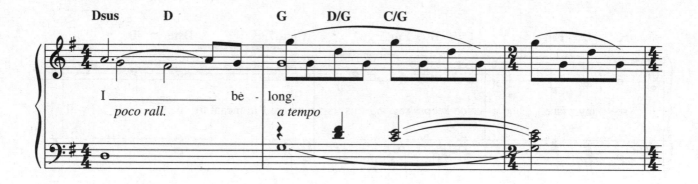

I _____ be - long.

poco rall.   *a tempo*

74

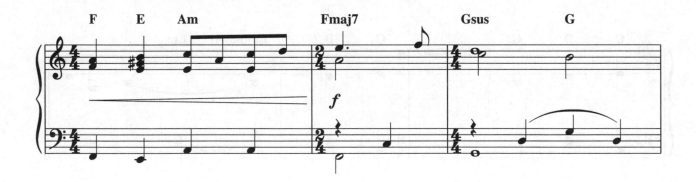

I am on my way. I can go the dis-tance. I don't

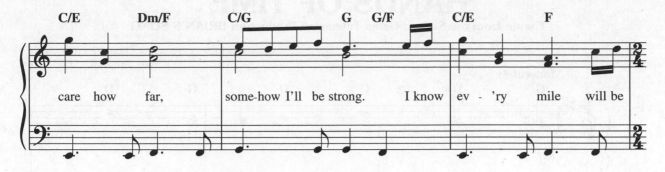

care how far, some-how I'll be strong. I know ev-'ry mile will be

worth my while. I would go most an - y - where to

find where I be - long.
poco rall. *a tempo*

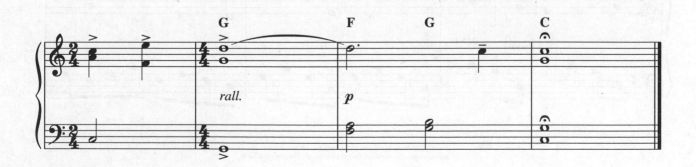

rall. *p*

HANDS OF TIME
Theme from the Screen Gems Television Production BRIAN'S SONG

Words by ALAN BERGMAN and MARILYN BERGMAN
Music by MICHEL LEGRAND

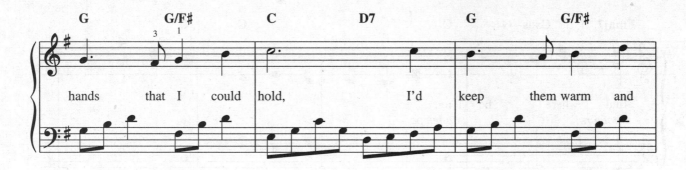

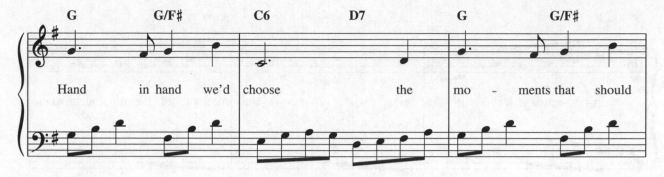

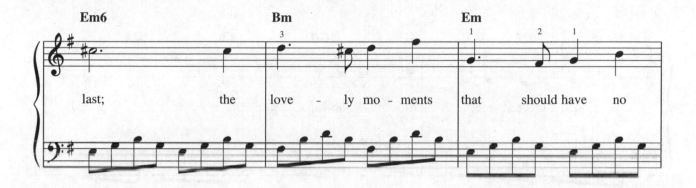

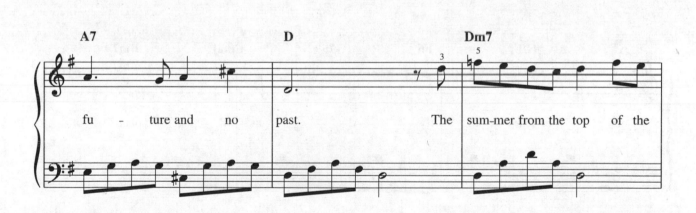

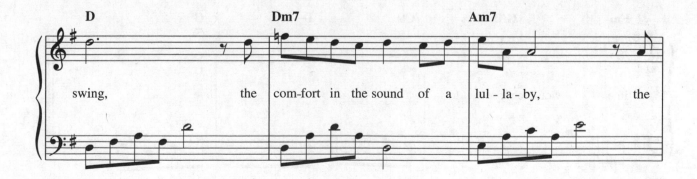

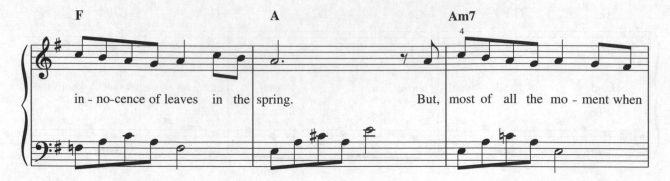

in - no-cence of leaves   in   the spring.   But, most of all the mo - ment when

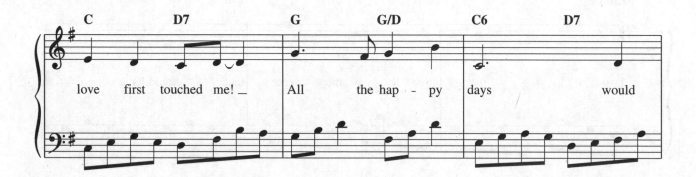

love   first touched me! _   All   the hap - py   days   would

nev - er learn   to   fly,   un - til   the hands   of

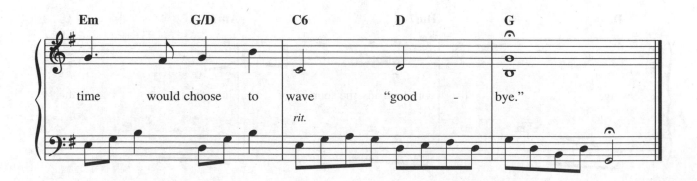

time   would choose to   wave   "good - bye."

I WANT TO SPEND MY LIFETIME LOVING YOU

from the TriStar Motion Picture THE MASK OF ZORRO

Music by JAMES HORNER
Lyric by WILL JENNINGS

80

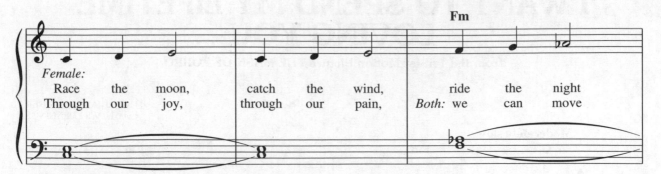

Female:
Race the moon, catch the wind, ride the night
Through our joy, through our pain, *Both:* we can move

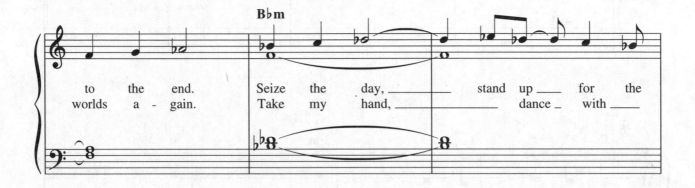

to the end. Seize the day, _____ stand up _____ for the
worlds a - gain. Take my hand, _____ dance _ with _____

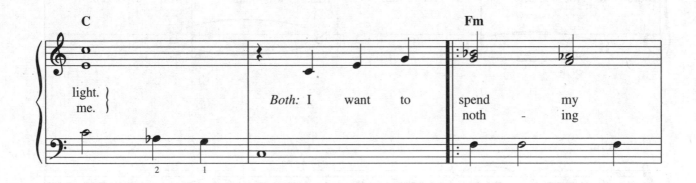

light.
me. } *Both:* I want to spend my
noth - ing

life - time lov - ing you, if that is
else to see me through if I can

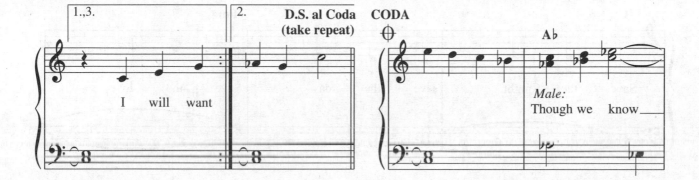

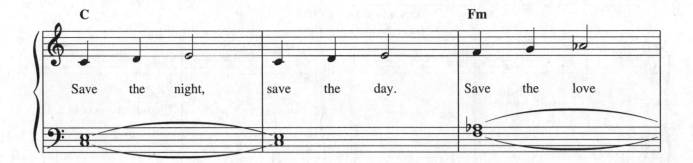

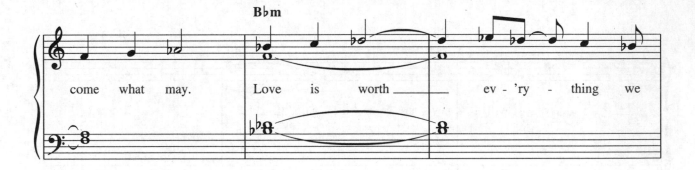

life - time / else   to   lov - ing you / see me through   if that is / if   I   can

1.,2.
Fm

all   in   life   I   ev - er   do.

3.
Bbm

I   want   to   spend   my   life - time
I   will   want   *rit.*

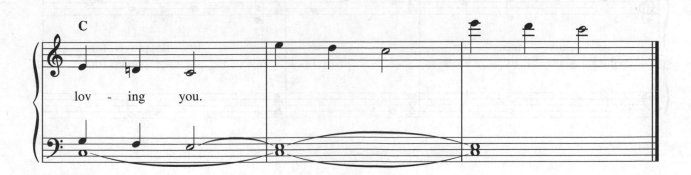

C

lov - ing   you.

I SAY A LITTLE PRAYER

featured in the TriStar Motion Picture MY BEST FRIEND'S WEDDING

Lyric by HAL DAVID
Music by BURT BACHARACH

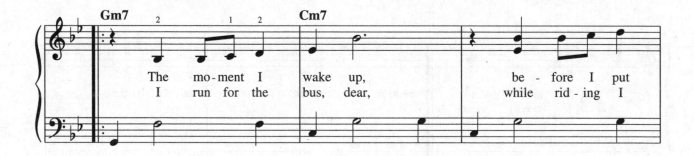

The mo-ment I wake up, before I put
I run for the bus, dear, while rid-ing I

on my make-up ___ I say a lit-tle prayer for
think of us, dear. ___ I say a lit-tle prayer for

85

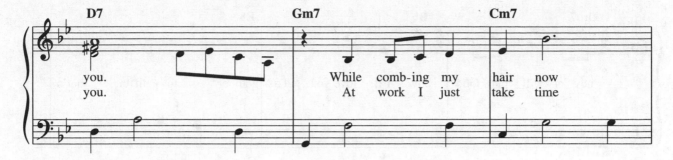

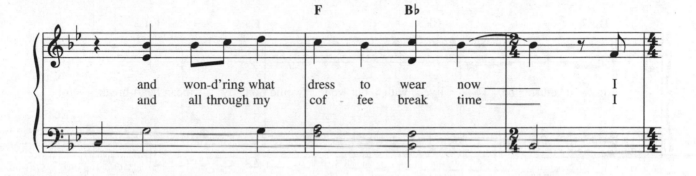

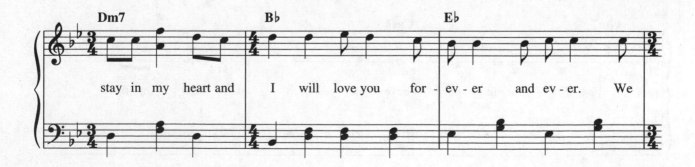

nev-er will part. Oh, how I'll love you. To-geth-er, to-geth-er, that's

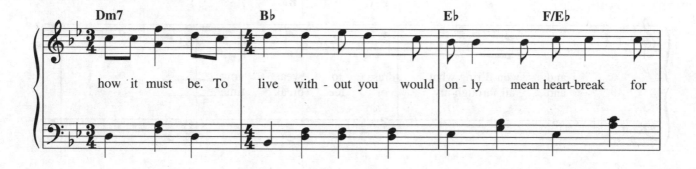

how it must be. To live with-out you would on-ly mean heart-break for

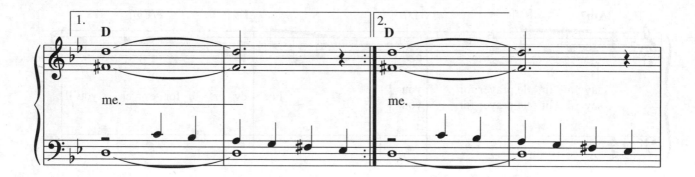

me. ____ me. ____

My dar-ling, be-lieve me, for me there is

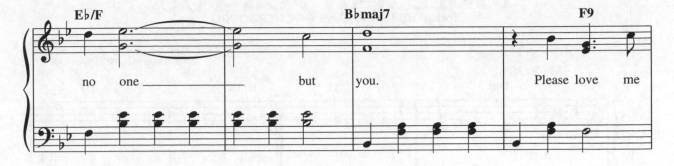

no one _____ but you. Please love me

too. _____ I'm in love with you. _____

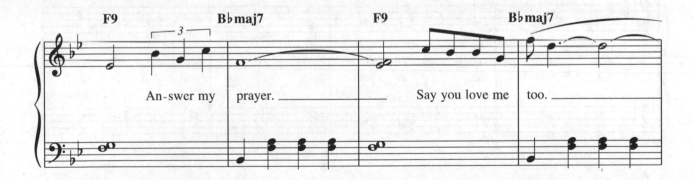

An-swer my prayer. _____ Say you love me too. _____

rit.

I WILL WAIT FOR YOU
from THE UMBRELLAS OF CHERBOURG

Music by MICHEL LEGRAND
Original French Text by JACQUES DEMY
English Words by NORMAN GIMBEL

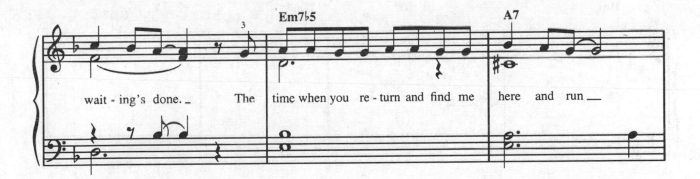

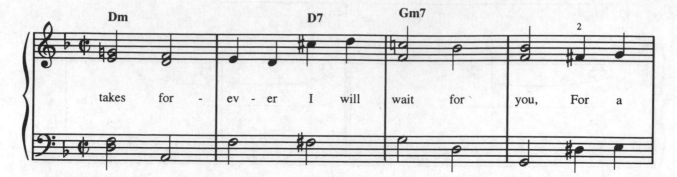

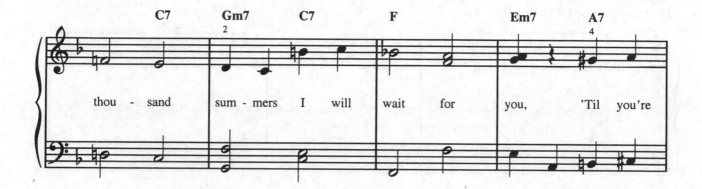

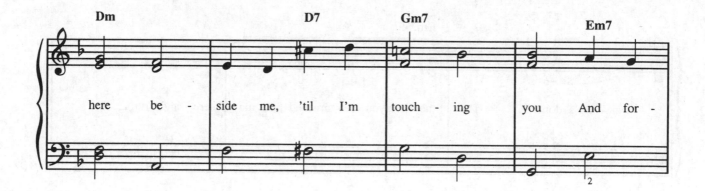

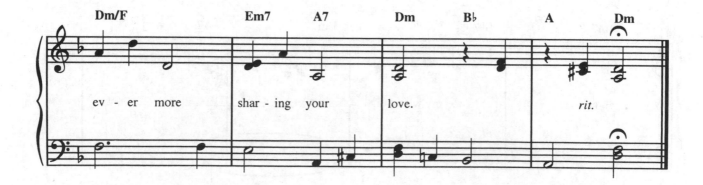

JAILHOUSE ROCK

featured in the Motion Picture THE BLUES BROTHERS

Words and Music by JERRY LEIBER
and MIKE STOLLER

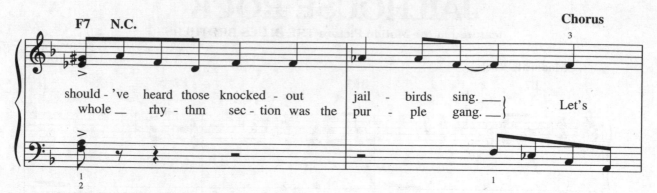

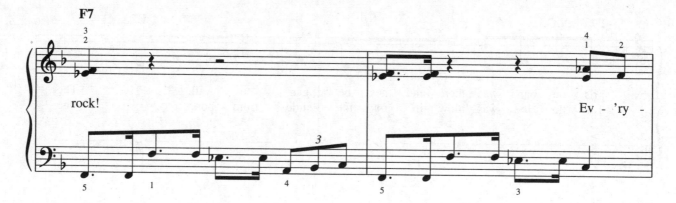

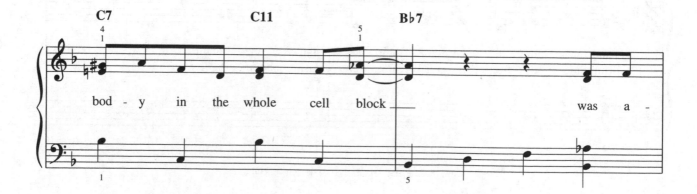

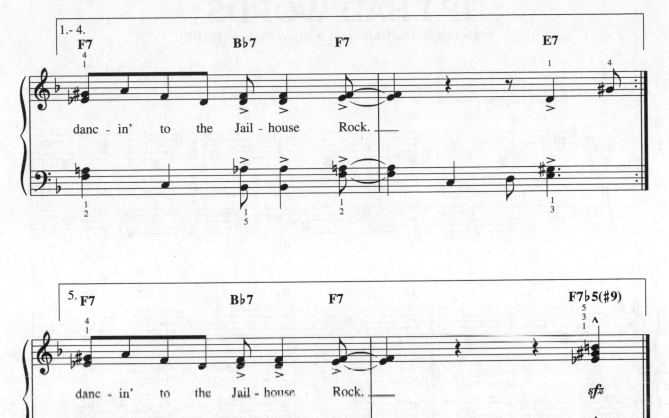

Additional Lyrics

3. Number Forty-seven said to Number Three:
   You're the cutest jailbird I ever did see.
   I sure would be delighted with your company.
   Come on and do the Jailhouse Rock with me.
   To Chorus:

4. The sad sack was a-sittin' on a block of stone,
   Way over in the corner weeping all alone.
   The warden said: Hey, buddy, don't you be no square.
   If you can't find a partner, find a wooden chair!
   To Chorus:

5. Shifty Henry said to Bugs: For heaven's sake.
   No one's lookin'; now's our chance to make a break.
   Bugsy turned to Shifty and said: Nix, nix:
   I wanna stick around a while and get my kicks.
   To Chorus:

IF I HAD WORDS
featured in the Universal Motion Picture BABE

By JOHN HODGE

Bright Reggae

If I had words to

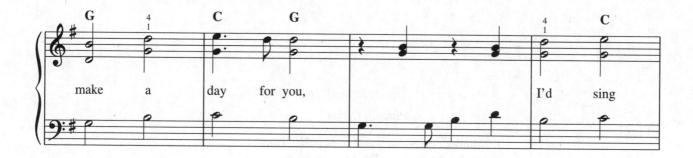

make a day for you, I'd sing

you a morn - ing gold - en and new.

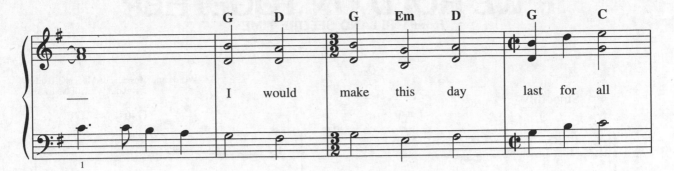

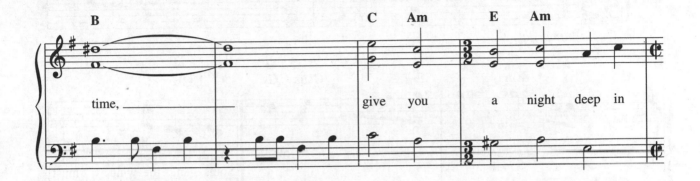

I would make this day last for all

time, _____ give you a night deep in

moon - shine. _____ shine. _____

IF WE HOLD ON TOGETHER
from THE LAND BEFORE TIME

Words and Music by JAMES HORNER
and WILL JENNINGS

Don't lose your way   with
Souls in the wind   must

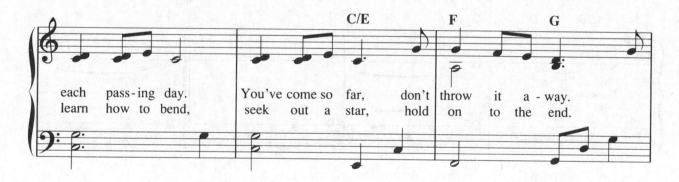

each pass-ing day.   You've come so far,   don't throw it a - way.
learn how to bend,   seek out a star,   hold on to the end.

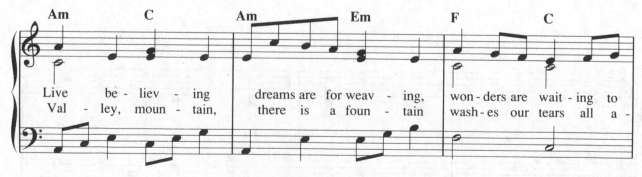

Live   be - liev - ing   dreams are for weav - ing,   won - ders are wait - ing to
Val - ley, moun - tain,   there is a foun - tain   wash - es our tears all a -

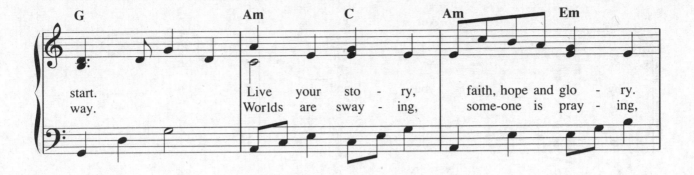

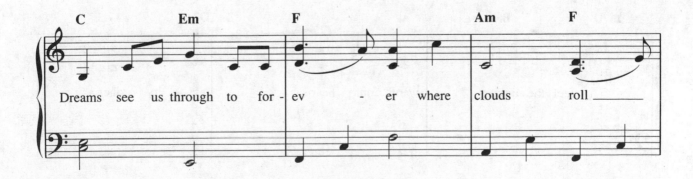

98

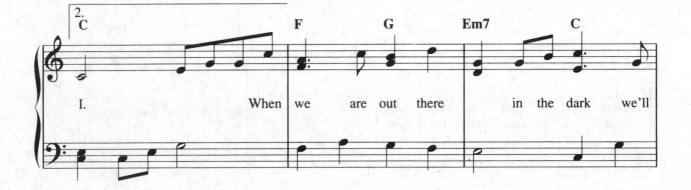

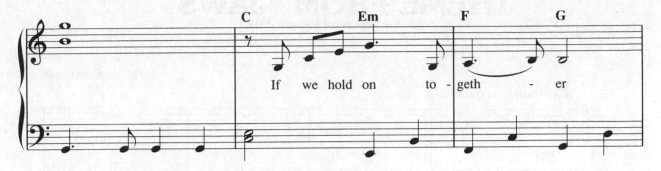

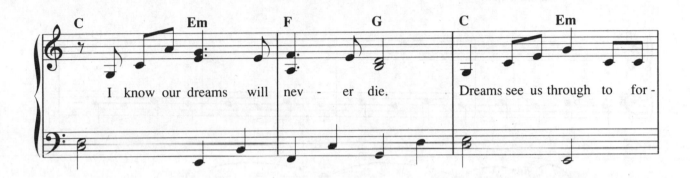

If we hold on to - geth - er

I know our dreams will nev - er die. Dreams see us through to for -

ev - er as high as souls can fly, the clouds roll

by for you and I.

THEME FROM "JAWS"

from the Universal Picture JAWS

By JOHN WILLIAMS

Very steady and threatening

8va throughout

(Repeat and fade)

THEME FROM "JURASSIC PARK"

from the Universal Motion Picture JURASSIC PARK

Composed by
JOHN WILLIAMS

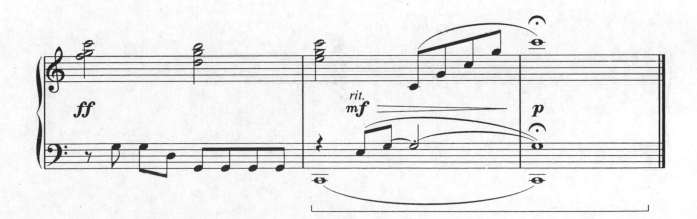

THEME FROM "LAWRENCE OF ARABIA"

from LAWRENCE OF ARABIA

By MAURICE JARRE

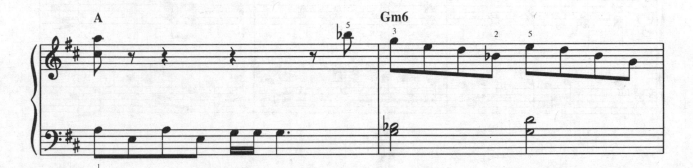

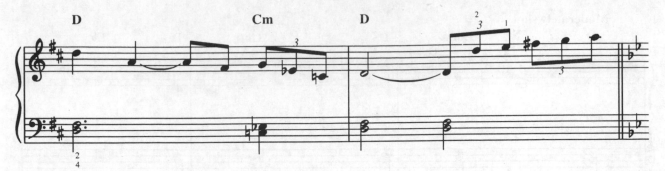

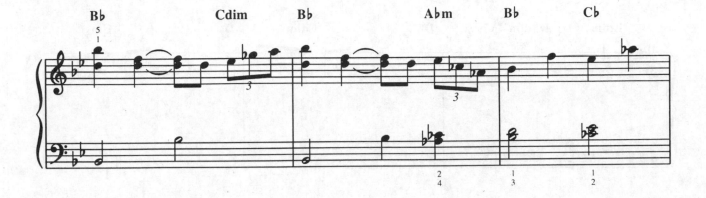

LEGENDS OF THE FALL

LEGENDS OF THE FALL

from TriStar Pictures' LEGENDS OF THE FALL

Composed by JAMES HORNER

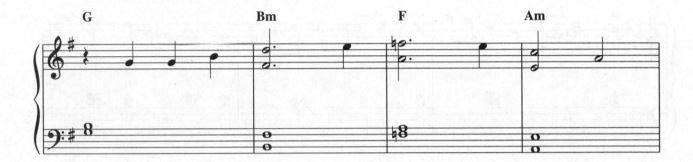

110

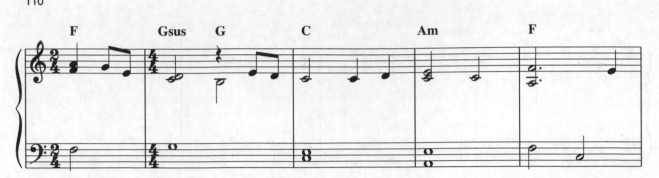

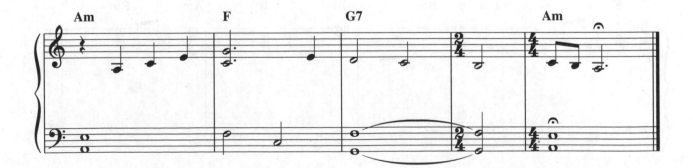

LET'S FACE THE MUSIC AND DANCE ¹¹¹

from the Motion Picture FOLLOW THE FLEET

Words and Music by
IRVING BERLIN

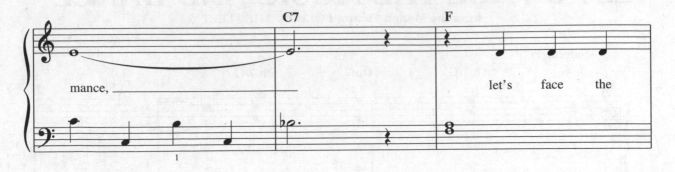

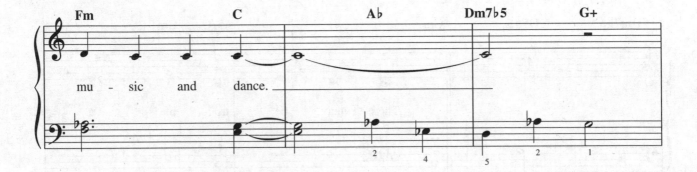

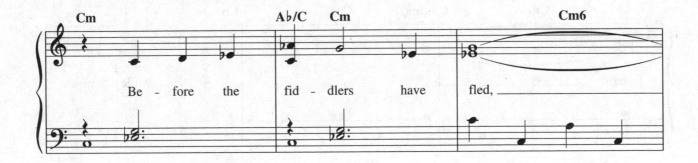

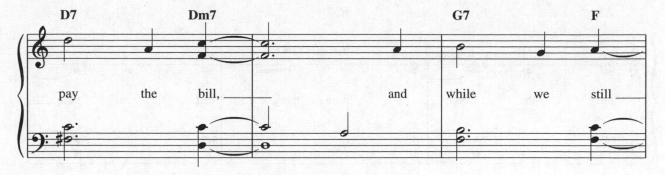

pay   the   bill,   and   while   we   still

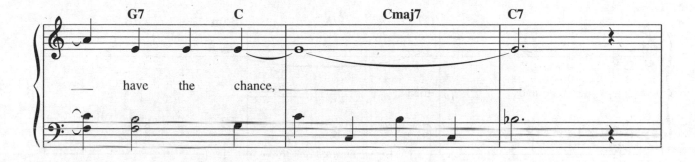

___   have   the   chance,

let's   face   the   mu - sic   and   dance.

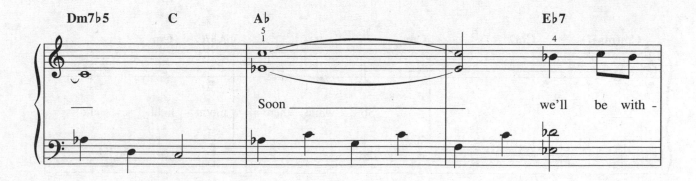

Soon   we'll   be   with -

114

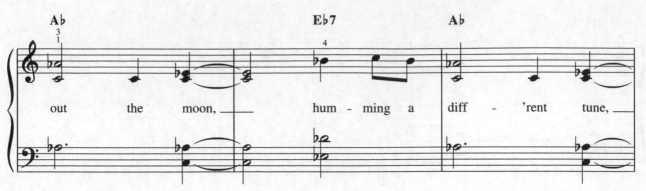

out   the   moon,   hum - ming a   diff - 'rent   tune,

and   then

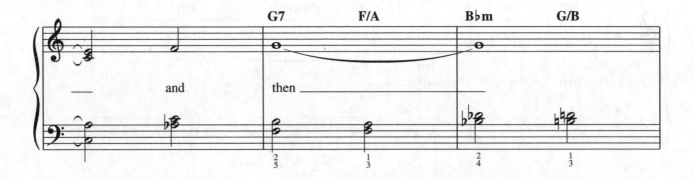

there   may   be   tear - drops   to   shed.

So   while   there's   moon - light   and

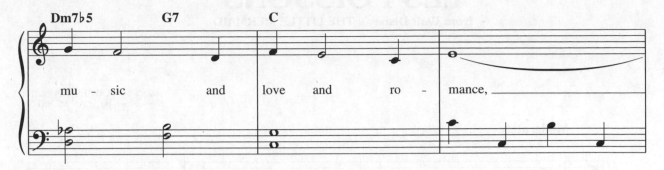

mu - sic and love and ro - mance,

let's face the mu - sic and dance,

dance. Let's face the

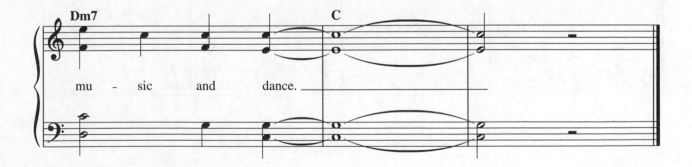

mu - sic and dance.

LES POISSONS
from Walt Disney's THE LITTLE MERMAID

Lyrics by HOWARD ASHMAN
Music by ALAN MENKEN

Moderately

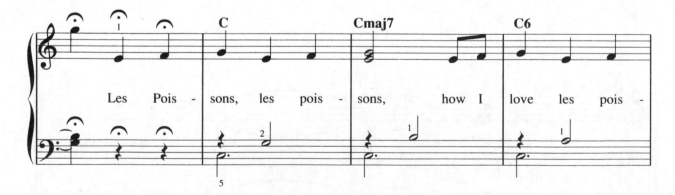

Les Pois - sons, les pois - sons, how I love les pois -

117

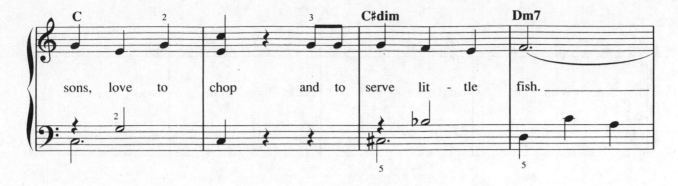

sons, love to chop and to serve lit - tle fish.

First I cut off their heads, then I pull out their

bones. Ah mais oui, ca c'est tou - jours de - lish.

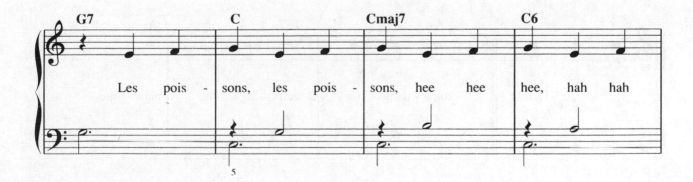

Les pois - sons, les pois - sons, hee hee hee, hah hah

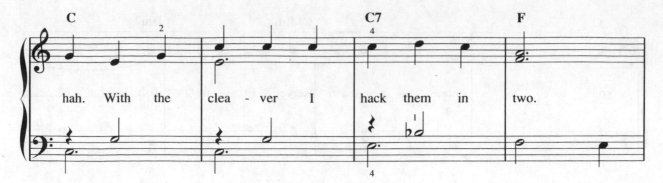

hah. With the clea - ver I hack them in two.

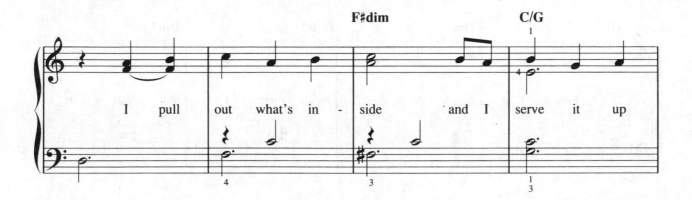

I pull out what's in - side and I serve it up

fried, God, I love lit - tle fish - es, don't you? _____

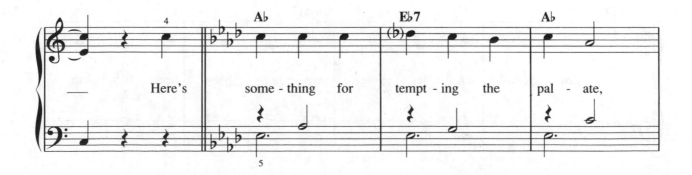

_____ Here's some - thing for tempt - ing the pal - ate,

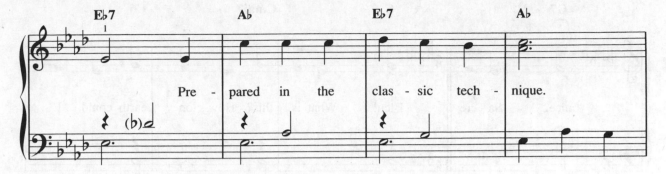

Pre- pared in the clas - sic tech - nique.

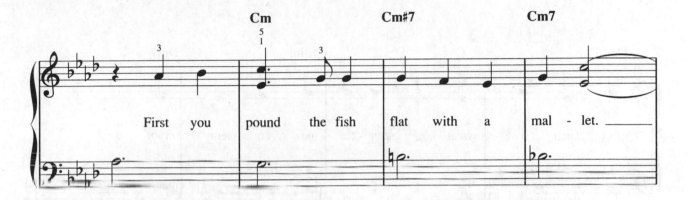

First you pound the fish flat with a mal - let. ____

____ Then you slash through the skin, give the bel - ly a

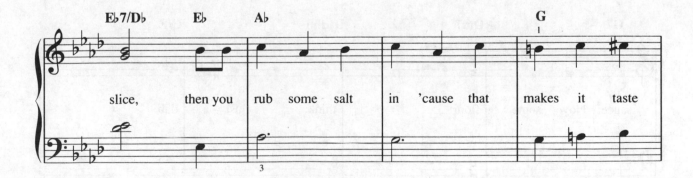

slice, then you rub some salt in 'cause that makes it taste

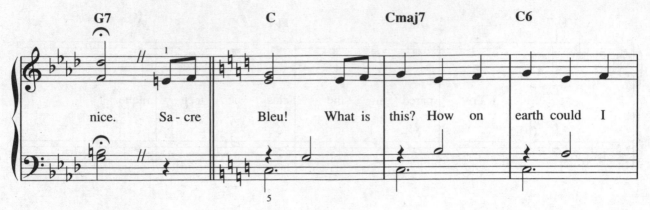

nice. Sa - cre Bleu! What is this? How on earth could I

miss such a sweet lit - tle suc - cu - lent crab.

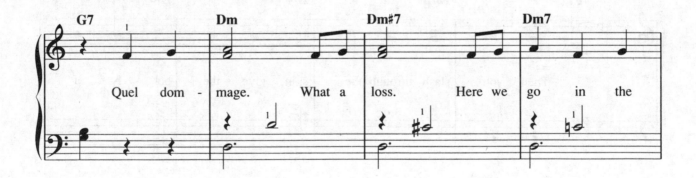

Quel dom - mage. What a loss. Here we go in the

sauce. Now some flour ____ I think, just a dab.

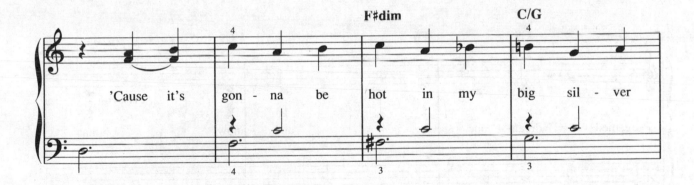

LONG AGO
(And Far Away)
from COVER GIRL

Words by IRA GERSHWIN
Music by JEROME KERN

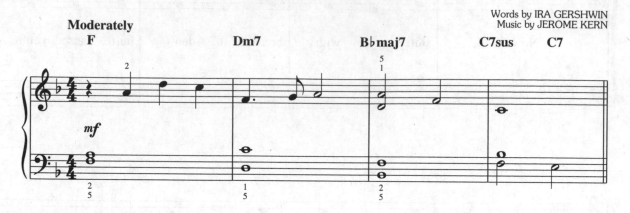

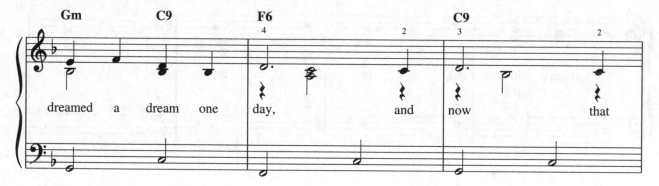

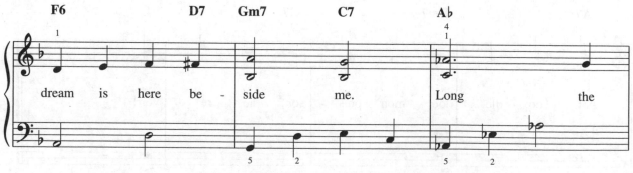

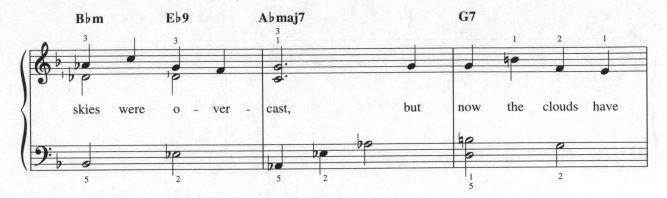

skies were o - ver - cast, but now the clouds have

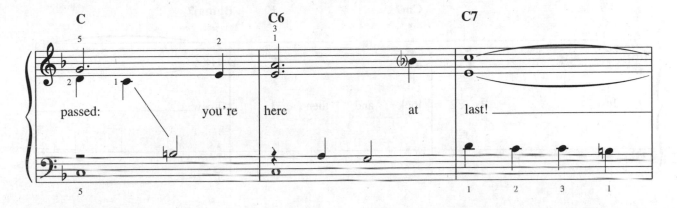

passed: you're here at last!

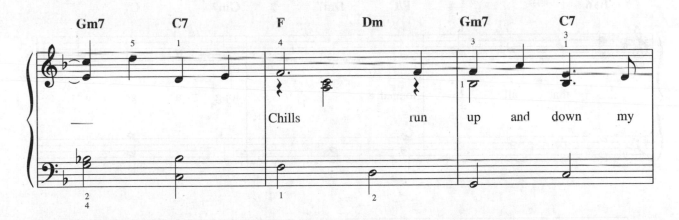

Chills run up and down my

spine, A - lad - din's lamp is mine, the

dream   I   dreamed was   not   de - nied   me.

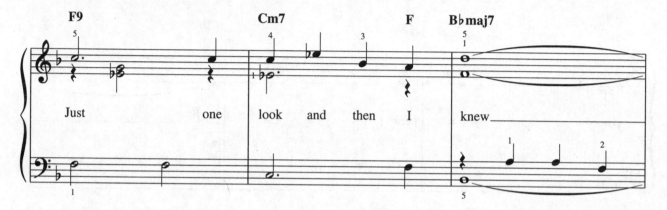

Just   one   look   and   then   I   knew_____

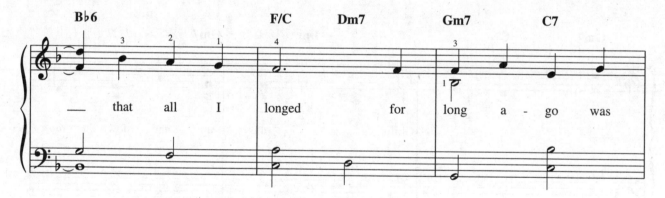

___ that   all   I   longed   for   long   a - go   was

you.   you.

THE LOOK OF LOVE
from CASINO ROYALE

Words by HAL DAVID
Music by BURT BACHARACH

Moderately

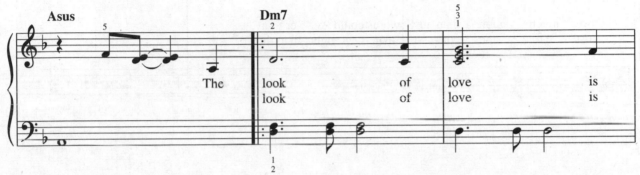

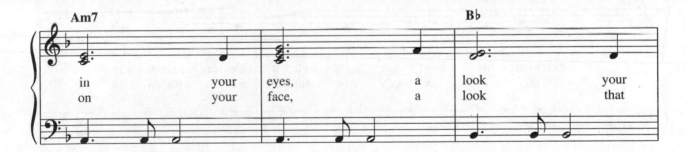

126

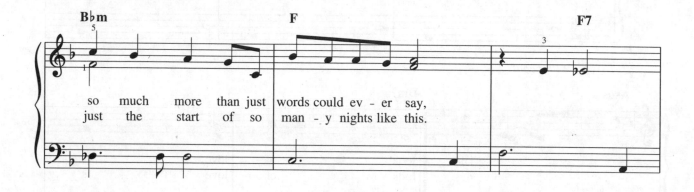

how long__ have I wait - ed, wait - ed just to love you now,__

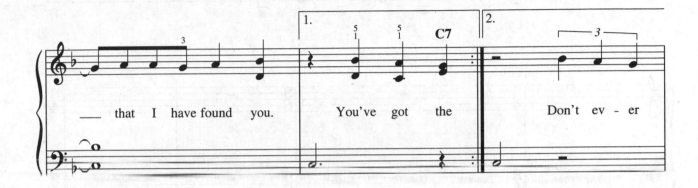

__ that I have found you. You've got the

Don't ev - er

go, don't ev - er go,

I love you so.

THEME FROM "THE LOST WORLD"

from the Universal Motion Picture THE LOST WORLD: JURASSIC PARK

Composed by JOHN WILLIAMS

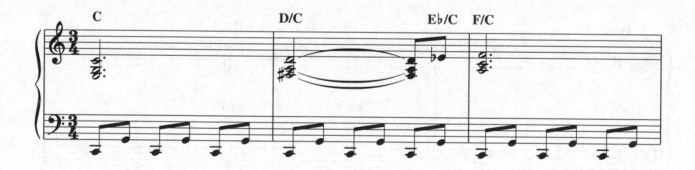

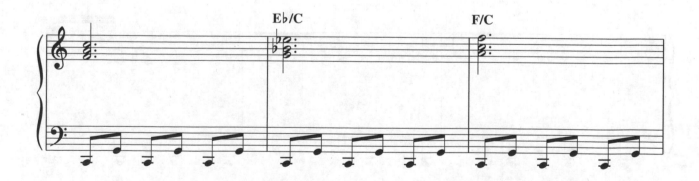

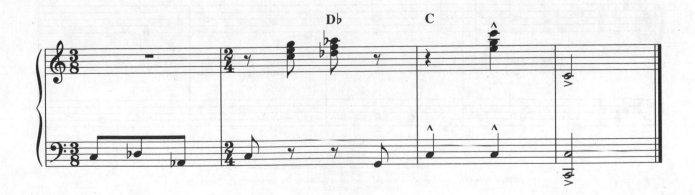

A MAN AND A WOMAN

(Un Homme et une Femme)
from A MAN AND A WOMAN

Original Words by PIERRE BAROUH
English Words by JERRY KELLER
Music by FRANCIS LAI

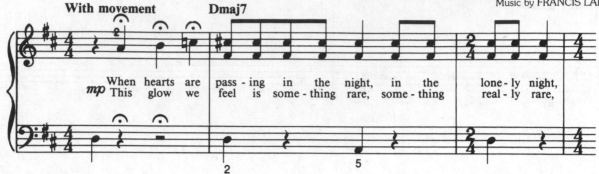

When hearts are pass-ing in the night, in the lone-ly night,
This glow we feel is some-thing rare, some-thing real-ly rare,

Then they must hold each oth-er tight, oh, so ver-y tight
So come and say you want to share, want to real-ly share

And take a chance that in the light, in to-mor-row's light,
The beau-ty wait-ing for us there, call-ing for us there

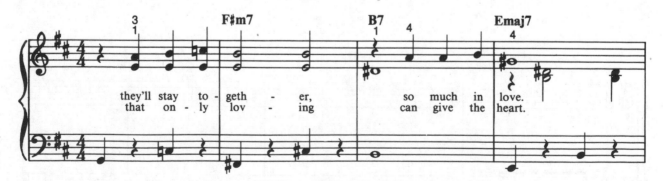

they'll stay to-geth-er, so much in love.
that on-ly lov-ing can give the heart.

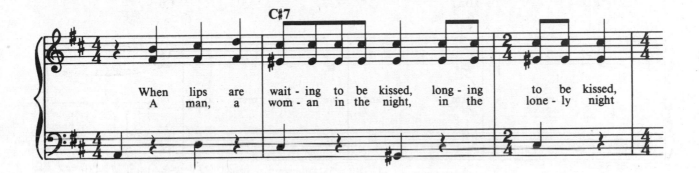

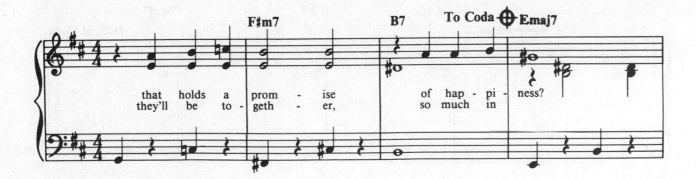

134

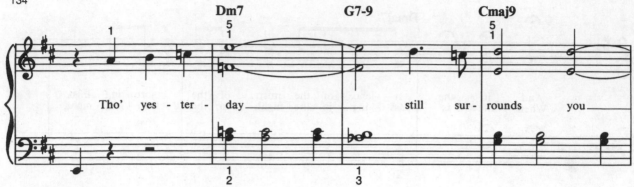

Tho' yes-ter-day _____ still sur-rounds you _____

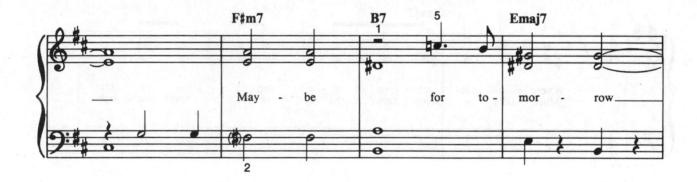

_____ with a warm and pre-cious mem-o-ry, _____

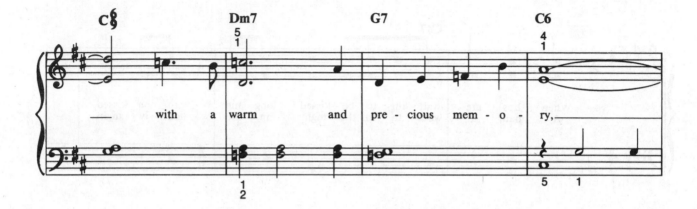

_____ May-be for to-mor-row _____

D.C. al Coda

_____ we can build a new dream for you and me.

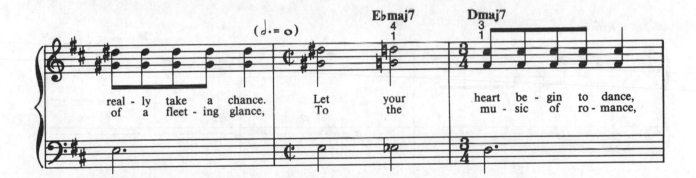

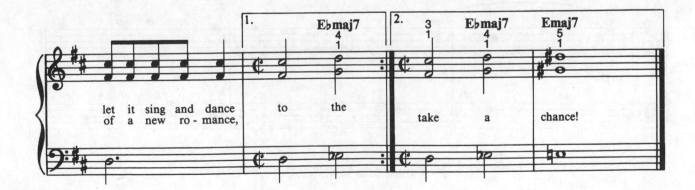

THE MUSIC OF GOODBYE
Love Theme from OUT OF AFRICA

Music by JOHN BARRY
Words by ALAN and MARILYN BERGMAN

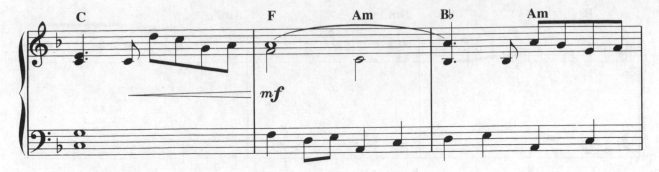

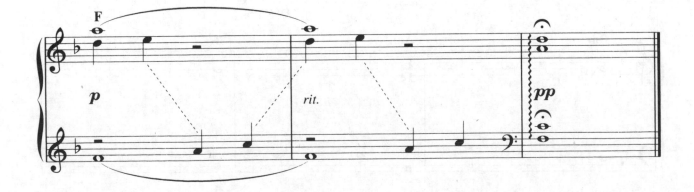

ON GOLDEN POND

Main Theme from ON GOLDEN POND

Music by DAVE GRUSIN

Very freely

p very delicately, as though from far away

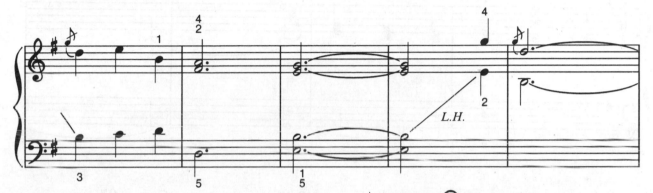

Not fast, somewhat freely

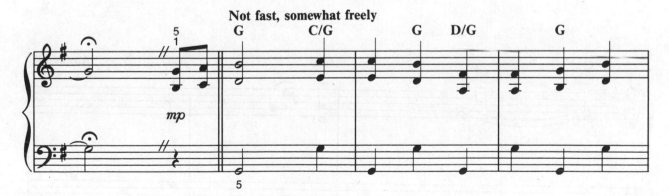

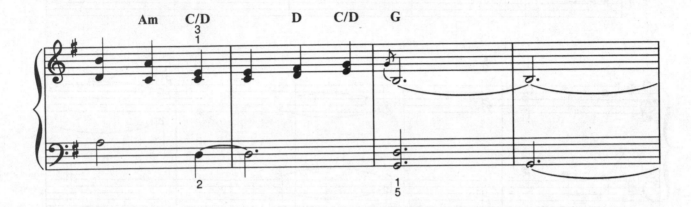

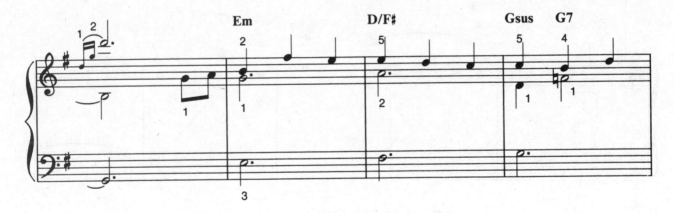

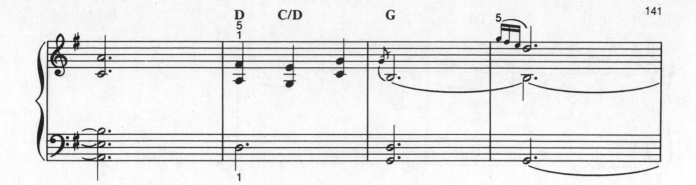

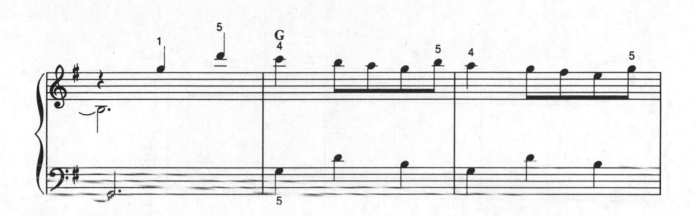

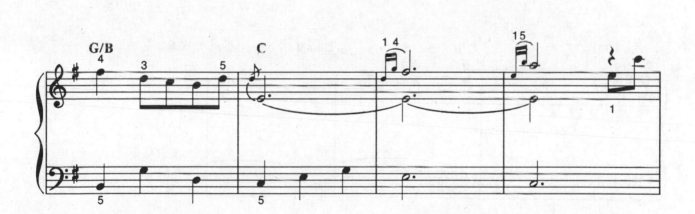

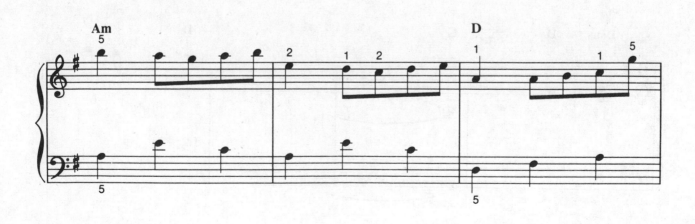

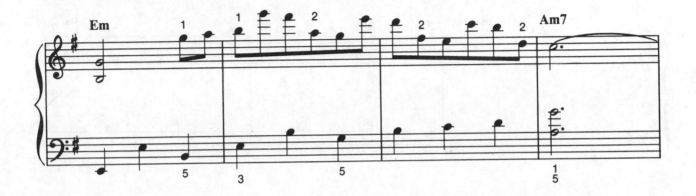

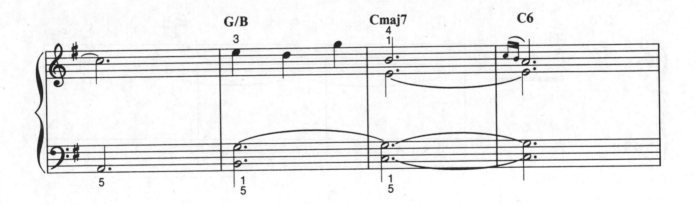

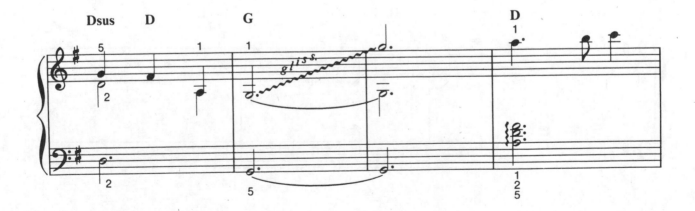

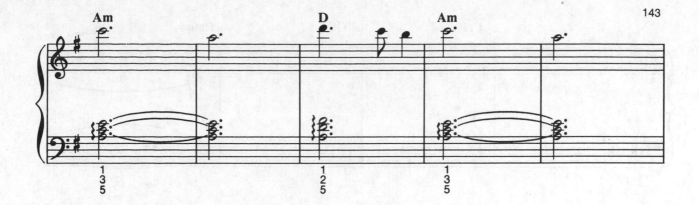

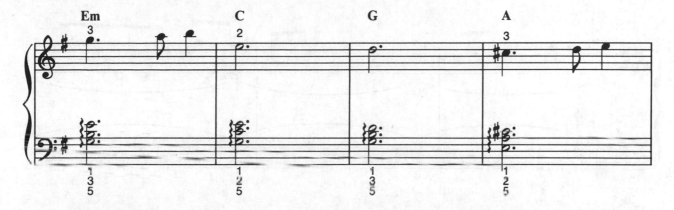

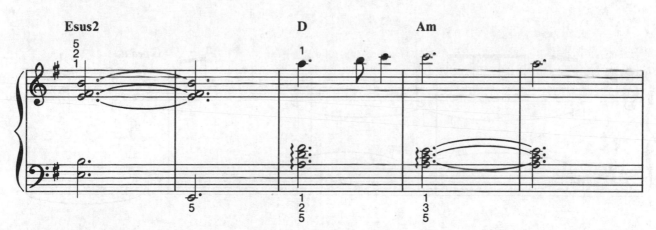

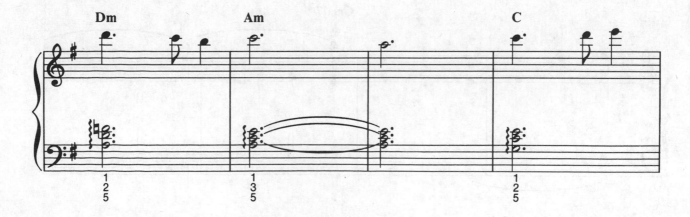

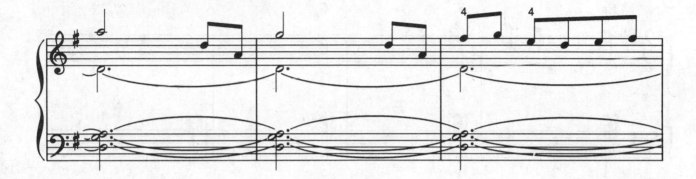

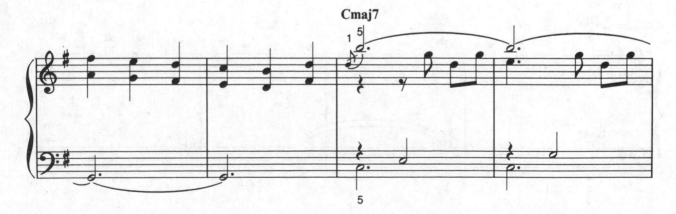

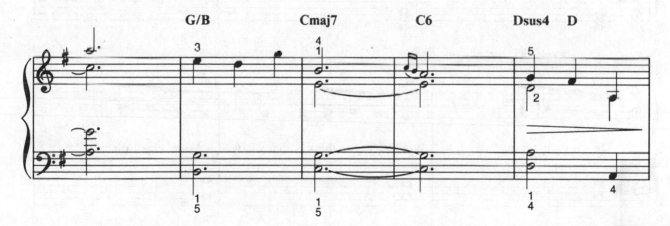

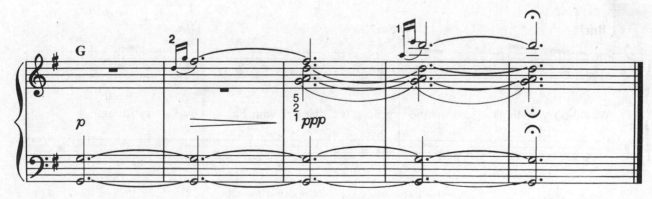

PART OF YOUR WORLD

from Walt Disney's THE LITTLE MERMAID

Lyrics by HOWARD ASHMAN
Music by ALAN MENKEN

Moderately

Look at this stuff. _

Is - n't it neat? _   Would-n't you think _ my col - lec-tion's com-plete? _

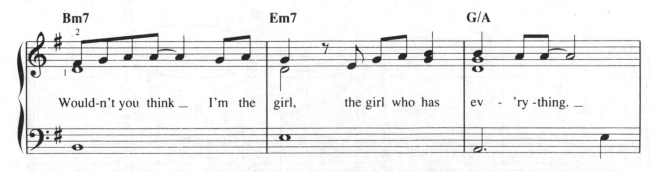

Would-n't you think _ I'm the girl, the girl who has ev - 'ry-thing. _

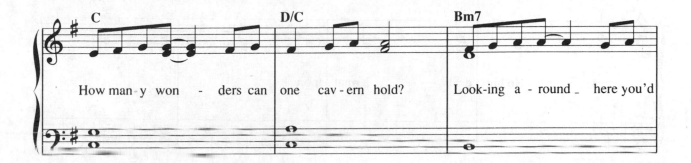

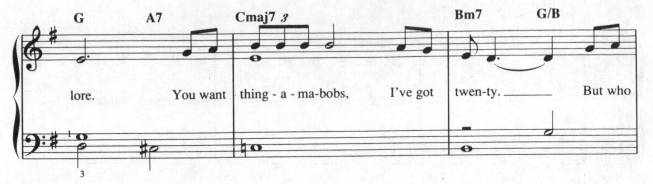

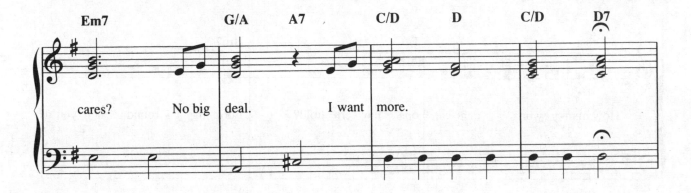

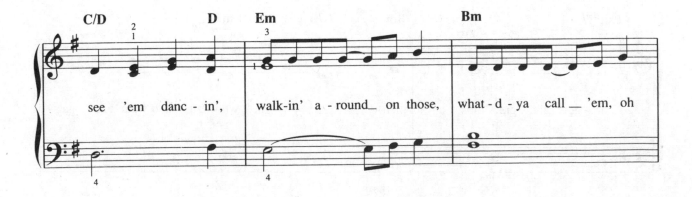

feet. Flip-pin' your fins __ you don't

get too far. Legs are re - quired __ for jump - in', danc - in'.

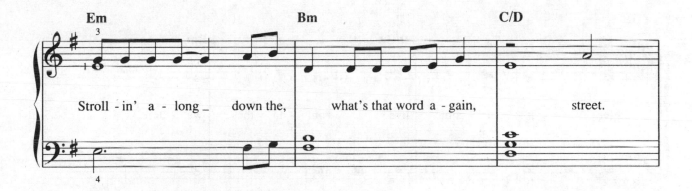

Stroll - in' a - long __ down the, what's that word a - gain, street.

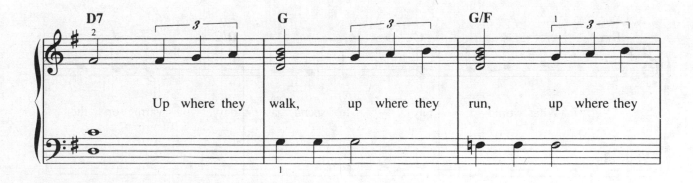

Up where they walk, up where they run, up where they

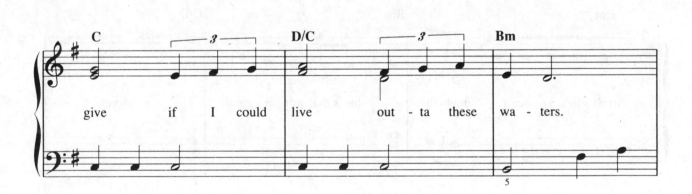

151

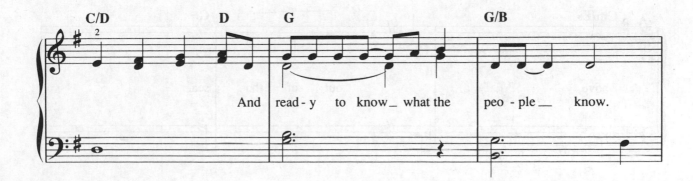

152

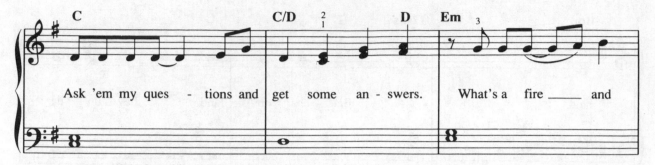

Ask 'em my ques - tions and get some an - swers. What's a fire _____ and

why does it, what's the word, burn. When's it my

turn? Would-n't I love, love to ex - plore that shore up a -

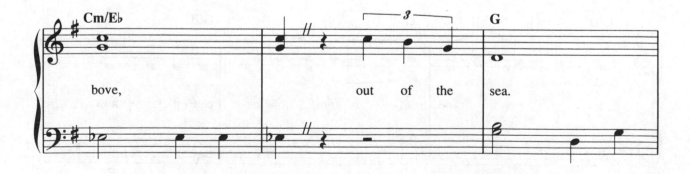

bove, out of the sea.

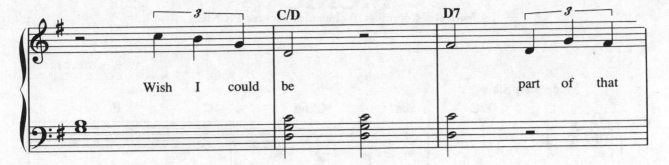

Wish I could be part of that

world.

PICNIC
from the Columbia Technicolor Picture PICNIC

Words by STEVE ALLEN
Music by GEORGE W. DUNING

Moderately Slow

On a pic - nic morn - ing, with - out a warn - ing, I looked at you and some - how I knew. On a day for sing - ing,

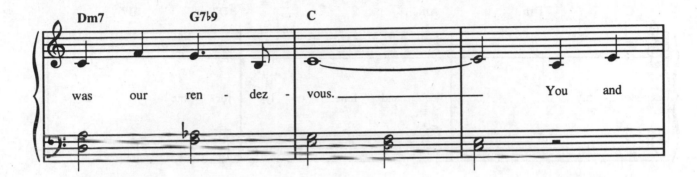

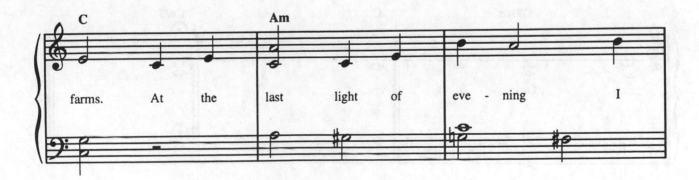

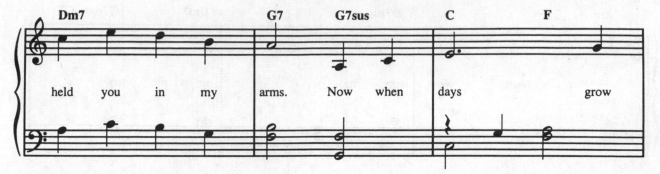

held you in my arms. Now when days grow

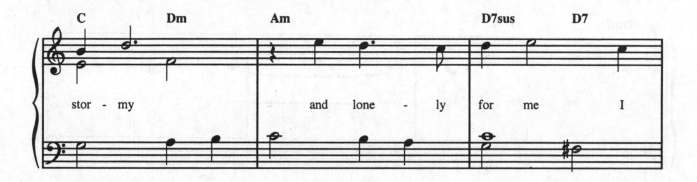

stor - my and lone - ly for me I

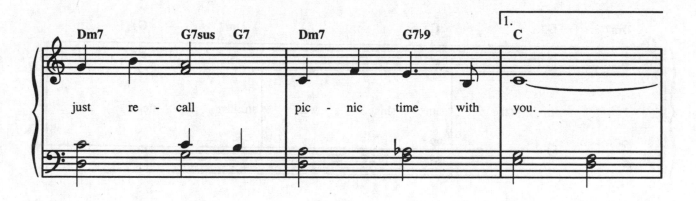

just re - call pic - nic time with you. ___

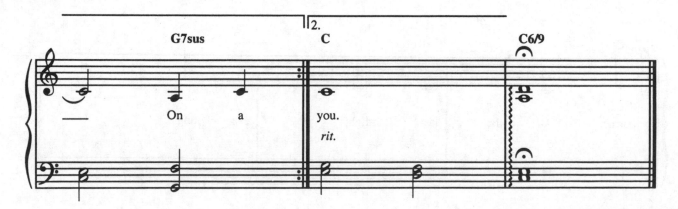

On a you.

rit.

PSYCHO
(Prelude)
Theme from the Paramount Picture PSYCHO

Music by BERNARD HERRMANN

Slightly agitated, rhythmic

PUTTIN' ON THE RITZ

from the Motion Picture PUTTIN' ON THE RITZ

Words and Music by
IRVING BERLIN

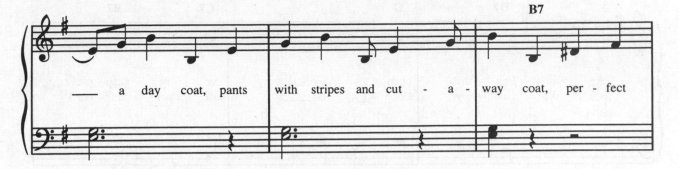

a day coat, pants with stripes and cut - a - way coat, per - fect

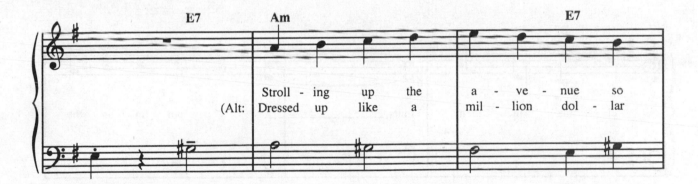

fits, _____ put - tin' on the Ritz.

Stroll - ing up the a - ve - nue so
(Alt: Dressed up like a mil - lion dol - lar

hap - py. _____   All dressed up just
troup - er. _____   Try - ing hard to

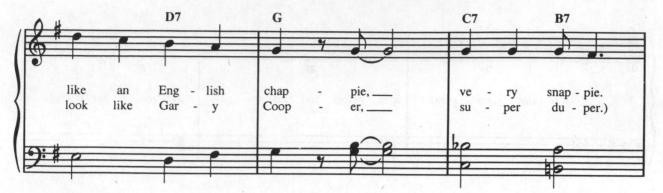

like an Eng - lish chap - pie, ___ ve - ry snap - pie.
look like Gar - y Coop - er, ___ su - per du - per.)

Come let's mix where Rock - e - fel - lers walk with sticks or "um - ber -

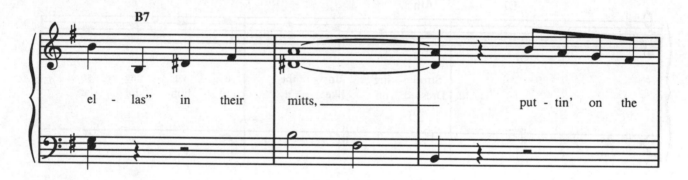

el - las" in their mitts, ___ put - tin' on the

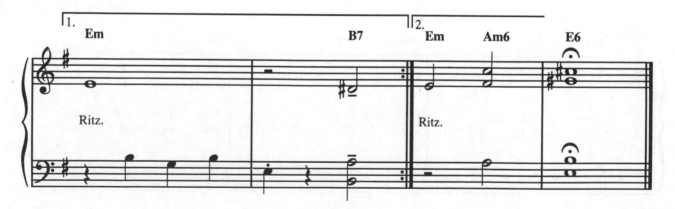

Ritz.   Ritz.

RAIDERS MARCH

from the Paramount Motion Picture RAIDERS OF THE LOST ARK

Music by JOHN WILLIAMS

March tempo

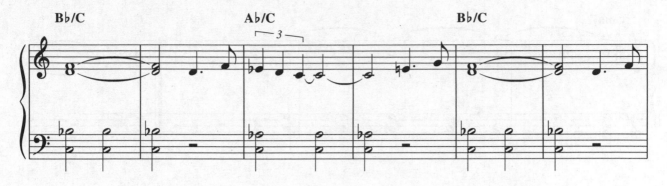

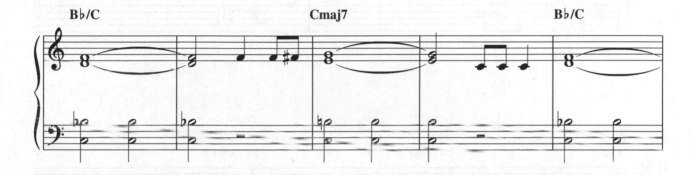

READY TO TAKE A CHANCE AGAIN

(Love Theme)
from the Paramount Picture FOUL PLAY

Words by NORMAN GIMBEL
Music by CHARLES FOX

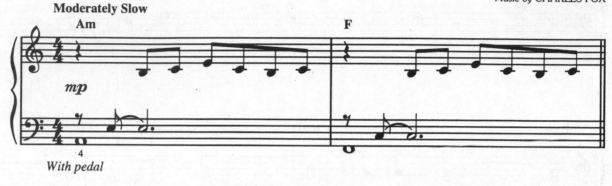

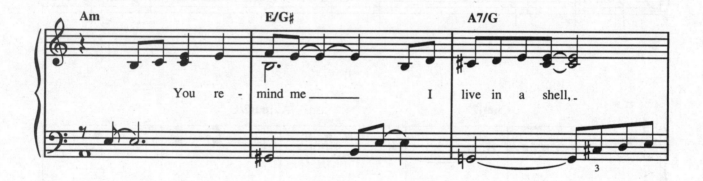

You re - mind me _____ I live in a shell,

Safe from the past, and do - in' o - kay, _____ but not ver - y well.

173

No jolts_ no sur-

pris - es, No cri - sis a - ris - es; My life_ goes a -

long as it should,_ it's all ver-y nice,_ but not ver-y good._

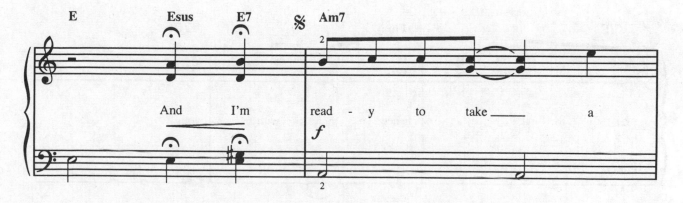

And I'm read-y to take_____ a

chance a - gain, _ Read - y to put _ my love on the line _ with

you. Been liv - ing with noth - ing to show _ for it; You

get what you get _ when you go _ for it, And I'm

read - y to take _ a chance a - gain _ with _ you.

When she left me _____ in

all my de - spair, _____ I just held on, My hopes were all

gone, _____ Then I found you there. And I'm

read - y to take _ a chance a - gain, _ Read - y to take _ a

chance a - gain — with — you, — With

you.

Repeat and Fade

RIVER
from the Motion Picture THE MISSION

Music by ENNIO MORRICONE

178

no - stra sic cla - ment. Vi - ta vi - ta no - stra tel - lus

no - stra vi - ta no - stra sic cla - ment.

Poe - na, poe - na no - stra vi - res no - stra poe - na

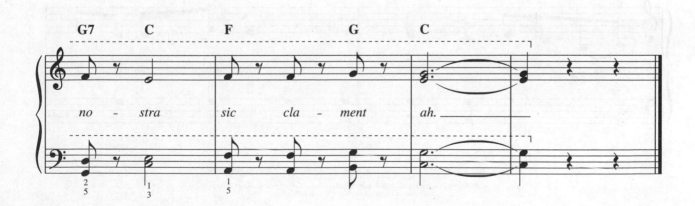

no - stra sic cla - ment ah.

REMEMBER ME THIS WAY

from the Universal Motion Picture CASPER

Music by DAVID FOSTER
Lyrics by LINDA THOMPSON

all, reach-es out each time you fall. You're the best friend that I've

found. ___ I know you ___ can't
And I know that you'll _ be

stay. But part of you ___ will nev - er, ev - er
there, for - ev - er - morc _ a part of me; you're

go a - way; your heart will stay.
ev - 'ry - where, I'll al - ways care.

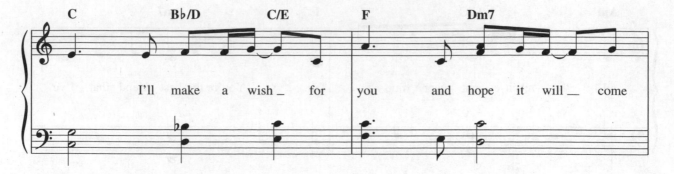

I'll make a wish _ for you and hope it will _ come

true: that life will just be kind to such a gen - tle

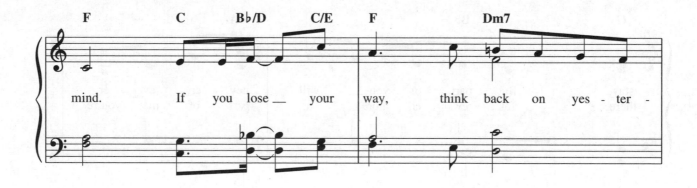

mind. If you lose _ your way, think back on yes - ter -

To Coda

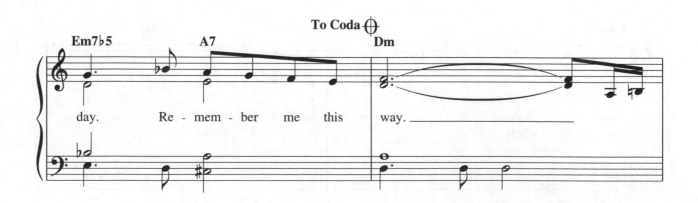

day. Re - mem - ber me this way. _____

F/G   G7   C/G   G7sus   G7

Re-mem-ber me this way.

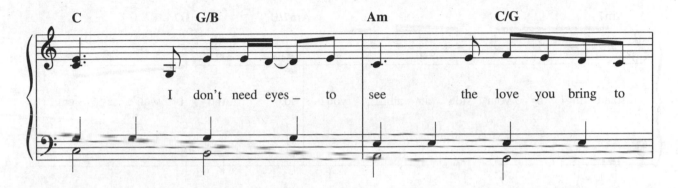

C   G/B   Am   C/G

I don't need eyes __ to see the love you bring to

D.S. al Coda

F   Dm7   G   Am7   G/B

me no mat-ter where __ I go.

CODA

Dm7   G7sus   G7   C

way. Re-mem-ber me this way. And I'll be

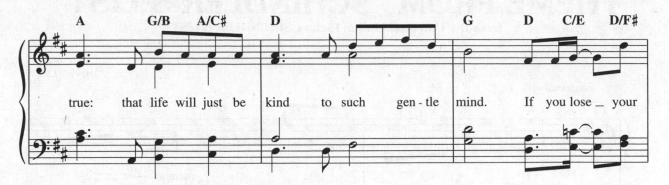

true: that life will just be kind to such gen-tle mind. If you lose _ your

way, think back on yes-ter-day. Re-mem-ber me this way. _____

Re-mem-ber me this way.

rit.   *a tempo*

molto rit.   This way. _____

THEME FROM "SCHINDLER'S LIST"

from the Universal Motion Picture SCHINDLER'S LIST

Music by
JOHN WILLIAMS

SEIZE THE DAY

from Walt Disney's NEWSIES

Lyrics by JACK FELDMAN
Music by ALAN MENKEN

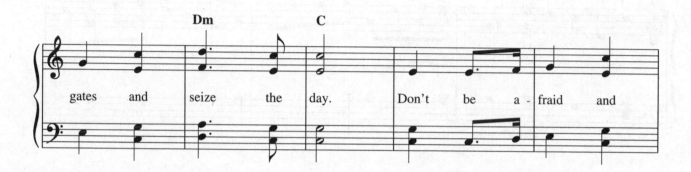

day.

David: Now is the time to seize the day.

Newsies: (Now is the time to seize the day.) *David:* Send out the call and join the fray.

Newsies: (Send out the call and join the fray.) *David:* Wrongs will _ be right - ed

if we're_ u - nit - ed. *All:* Let us ___ seize ___ the

day.

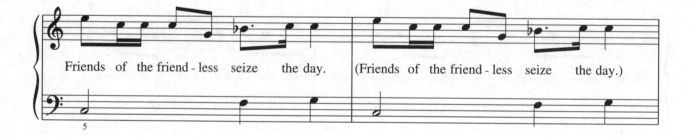

Friends of the friend - less seize the day. (Friends of the friend - less seize the day.)

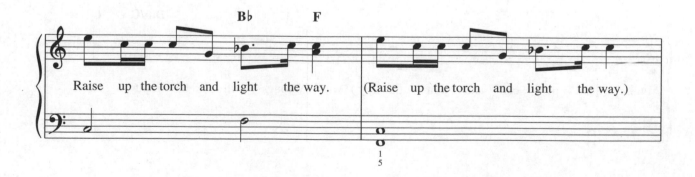

Raise up the torch and light the way. (Raise up the torch and light the way.)

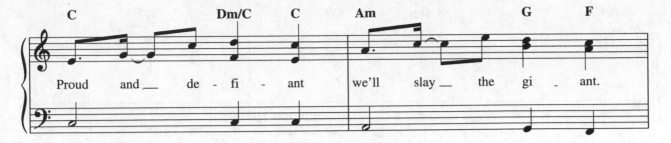

Proud and de - fi - ant we'll slay the gi - ant.

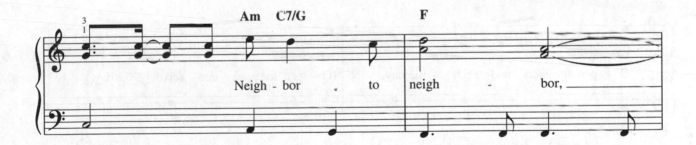

Let us seize the day.

Neigh - bor to neigh - bor,

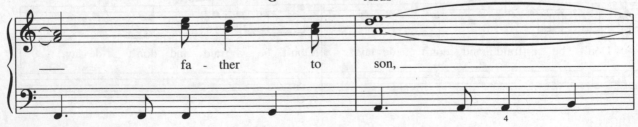

fa - ther to son,

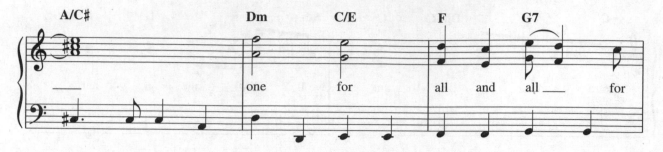

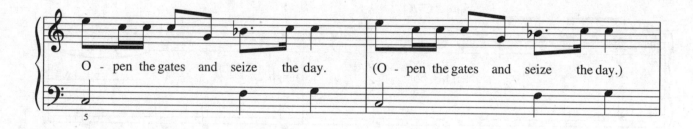

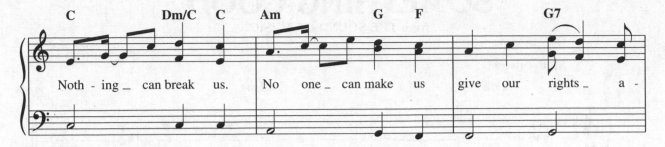

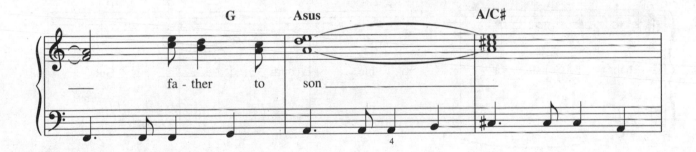

SOMETHING GOOD
from THE SOUND OF MUSIC

Lyrics and Music by
RICHARD RODGERS

Moderately

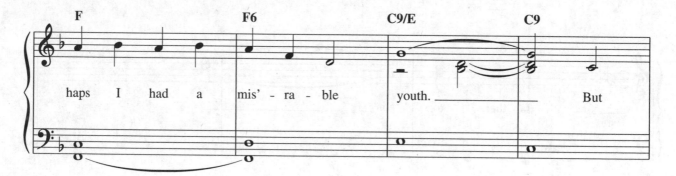

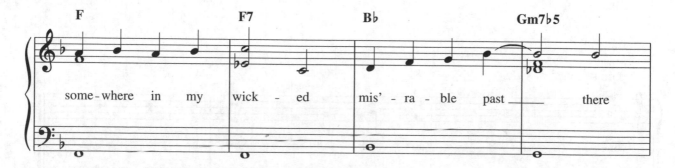

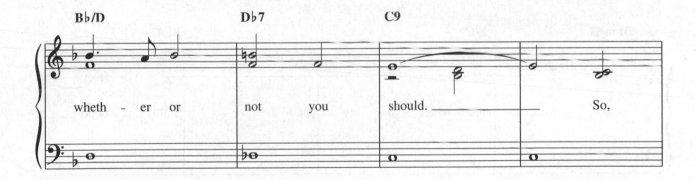

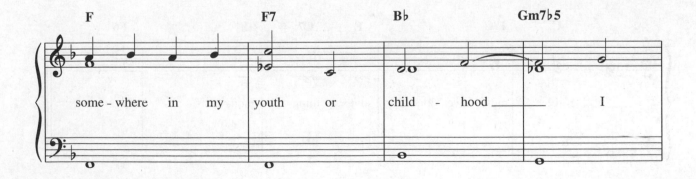

must have done   some - thing   good.   Per - good.

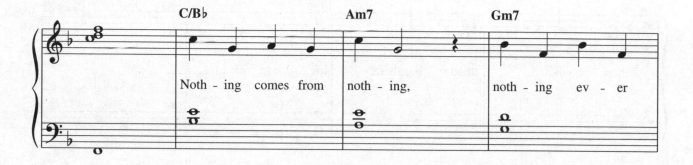

Noth - ing comes from   noth - ing,   noth - ing   ev - er

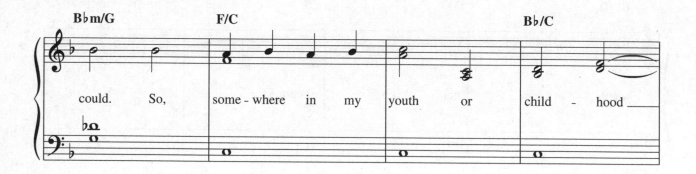

could.   So,   some - where   in   my   youth   or   child - hood

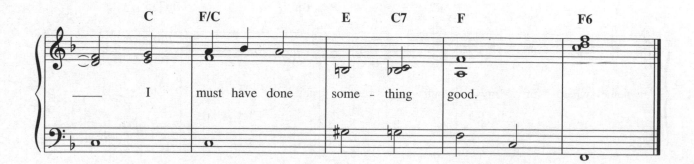

I   must have done   some - thing   good.

STEPPIN' OUT WITH MY BABY

from the Motion Picture Irving Berlin's EASTER PARADE

Words and Music by
IRVING BERLIN

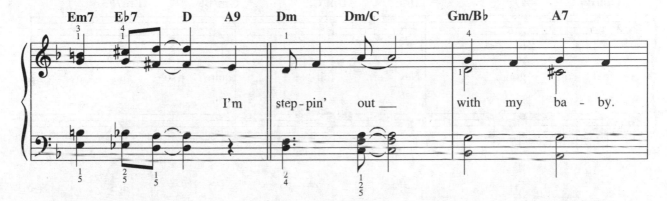

I'm step-pin' out ___ with my ba - by.

Can't go wrong ___ 'cause I'm in right. ___ It's for sure, ___

not for may - be, that I'm all dressed up to - night. ___

Steppin' out ___ with my hon-ey, can't be bad ___ to

feel so good. ___ Nev-er felt ___ quite so sun-ny.

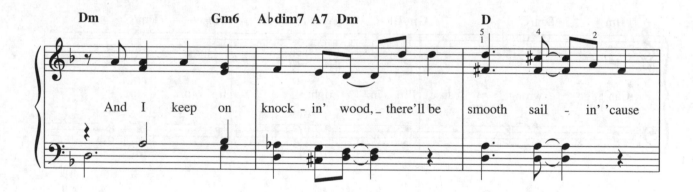

And I keep on knock-in' wood, ___ there'll be smooth sail-in' 'cause

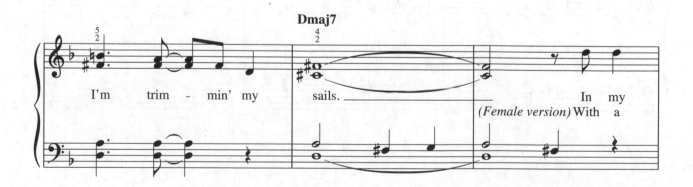

I'm trim-min' my sails. ___ In my
(Female version) With a

top   hat ___ and my   white   tie ___ and my   tails _____
bright shine ___ on my   shoes and ___ on my   nails _____

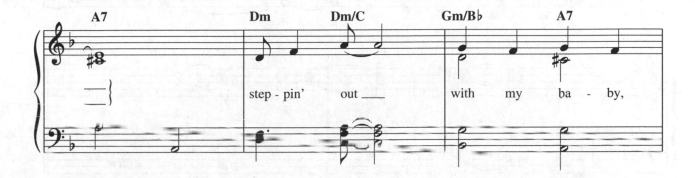

___   step - pin' out ___   with   my   ba - by,

can't go   wrong __ 'cause I'm in   right. __   Ask me   when __

will the   day   be,   the   big day may   be   to - night. _

SOMETHING TO TALK ABOUT

(Let's Give Them Something to Talk About)

from SOMETHING TO TALK ABOUT

Words and Music by
SHIRLEY EIKHARD

People are talk-ing, talk-ing a-bout peo-ple.
I feel so fool-ish. I nev-er no-ticed that,

I hear them whis-per, you won't be-lieve it.
ba-by, you're act-ing so nerv-ous like you're fall-ing.

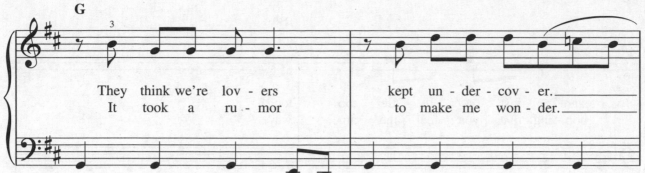

G

They think we're lov - ers
It took a ru - mor

kept un - der - cov - er.
to make me won - der.

D

I just ig - nore it.
Now I'm con - vinced that

They keep say - ing we
you're go - ing un - der, now.

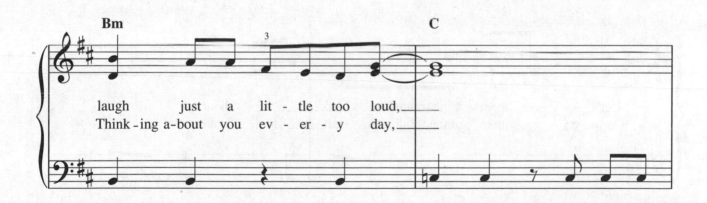

Bm

laugh just a lit - tle too loud,
Think - ing a - bout you ev - er - y day,

C

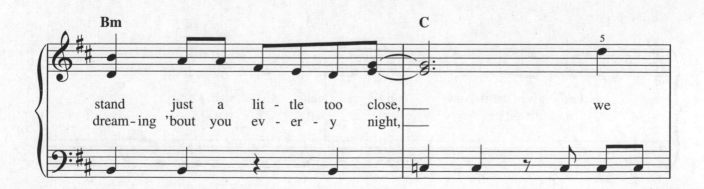

Bm

stand just a lit - tle too close,
dream - ing 'bout you ev - er - y night,

C

we

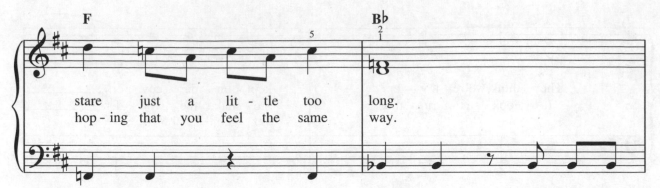

stare just a lit - tle too long.
hop - ing that you feel the same way.

May - be they're see - ing something we don't,_ dar - ling.
Now that we know it, let's real - ly show it, ba - by.

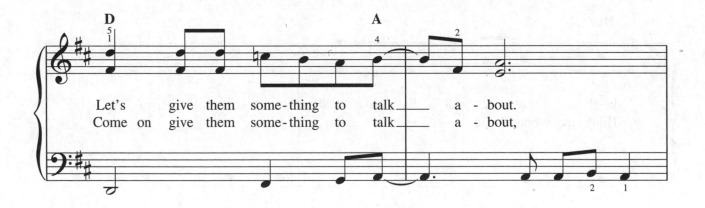

Let's give them some - thing to talk_ a - bout.
Come on give them some - thing to talk_ a - bout,

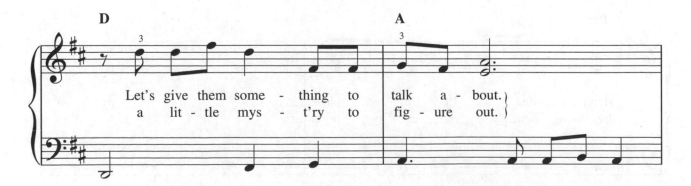

Let's give them some - thing to talk a - bout.
a lit - tle mys - t'ry to fig - ure out.

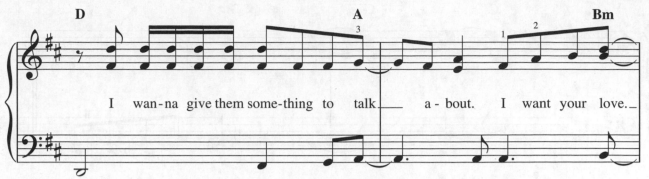

I wan-na give them some-thing to talk a-bout. I want your love.

And

Give a lit - tle some-thing to talk____ a - bout,__ babe.__

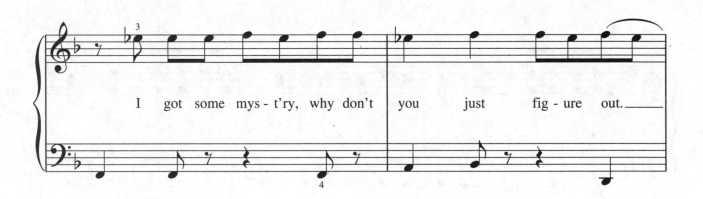

I got some mys - t'ry, why don't you just fig - ure out.____

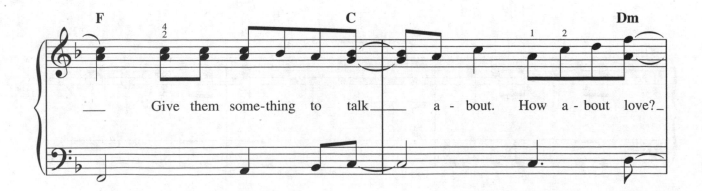

__ Give them some-thing to talk____ a - bout. How a - bout love?__

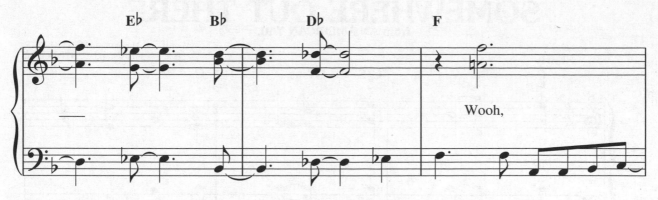

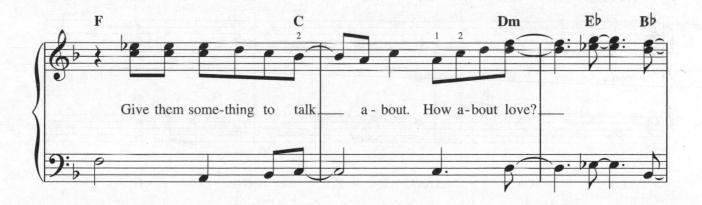

Somewhere Out There

from AN AMERICAN TAIL

Words and Music by JAMES HORNER,
BARRY MANN and CYNTHIA WEIL

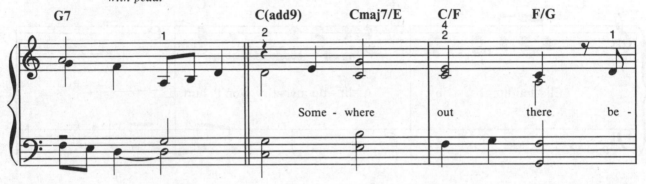

207

Some - where out there some - one's say - ing a prayer

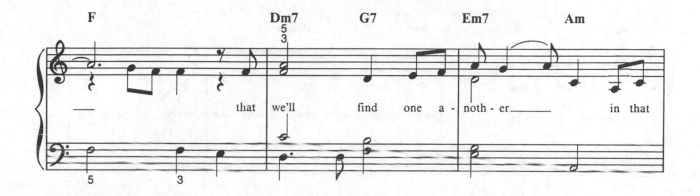

that we'll find one a - noth - er in that

big some - where out there. And e - ven though I know how ver - y

mf

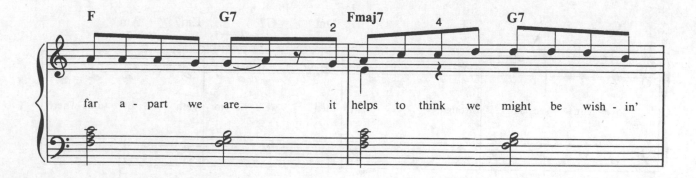

far a - part we are it helps to think we might be wish - in'

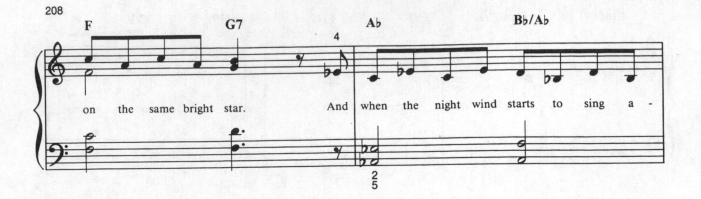

on the same bright star. And when the night wind starts to sing a-

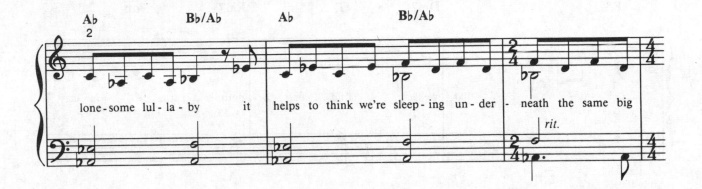

lone-some lul-la-by it helps to think we're sleep-ing un-der-neath the same big

sky. Some-where out there if

love can see us through, then we'll be to-geth-er some-where

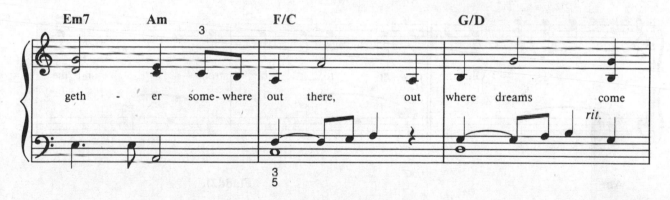

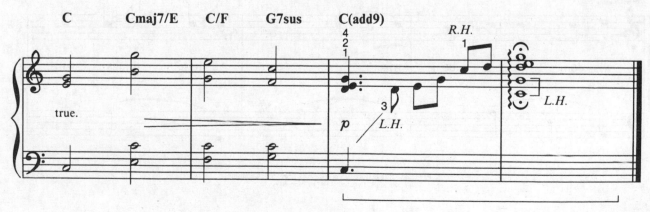

SON OF MAN

from Walt Disney Pictures' TARZAN™

Words and Music by
PHIL COLLINS

Moderately fast

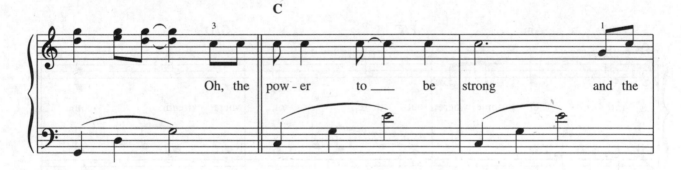

Oh, the pow-er to ___ be strong and the wis-dom to ___ be wise: ___ All these things ___ will

come to you _ in time. ___ On this jour-ney that _ you're
no one there _ to

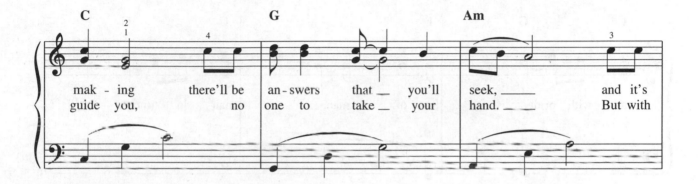

mak - ing there'll be an - swers that _ you'll seek, ___ and it's
guide you, no one to take _ your hand. ___ But with

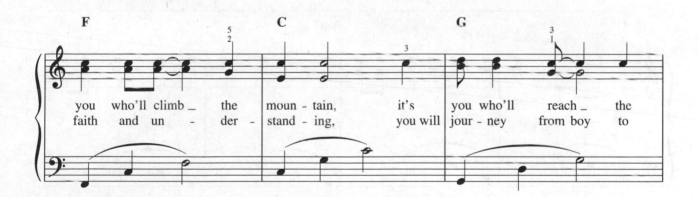

you who'll climb _ the moun - tain, it's you who'll reach _ the
faith and un - der - stand - ing, you will jour - ney from boy to

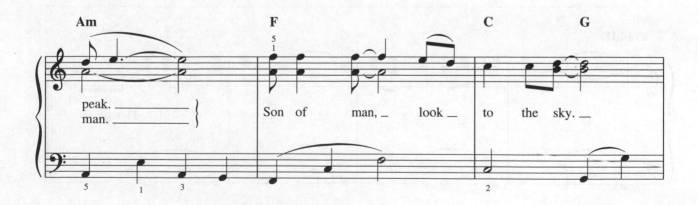

peak. ___ }
man. ___ }

Son of man, _ look _ to the sky. _

Lift your spir - it, set ___ it free. Some-day you'll ___ walk ___

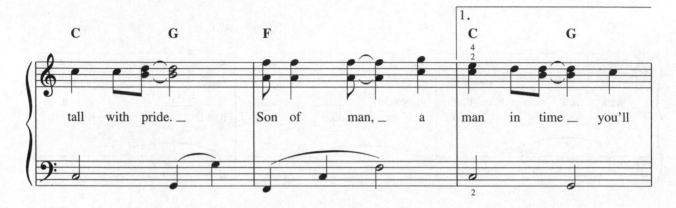

tall with pride. ___ Son of man, ___ a man in time ___ you'll

be. ___

Though there's

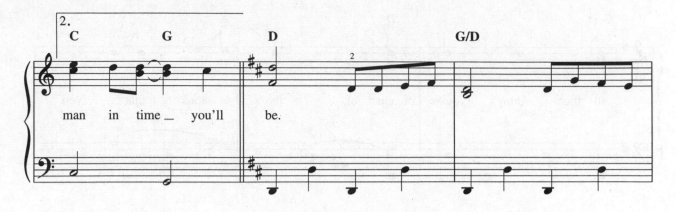

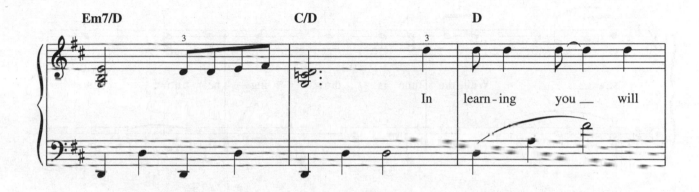

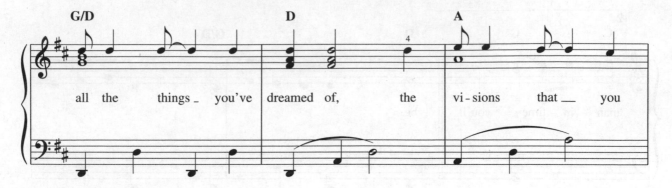

G/D   D   A

all the things you've dreamed of, the vi-sions that you

Bm   G/D   D

saw. _____ Well, the time is draw - ing near now; it's

A   Bm   G

yours to claim it all. _____ Son of man, look

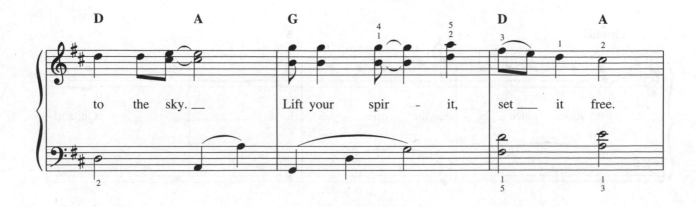

D   A   G   D   A

to the sky. _ Lift your spir - it, set it free.

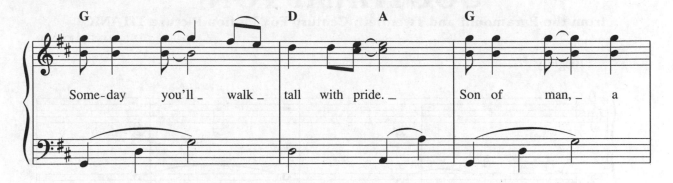

Some-day you'll_ walk_ tall with pride._ Son of man,_ a

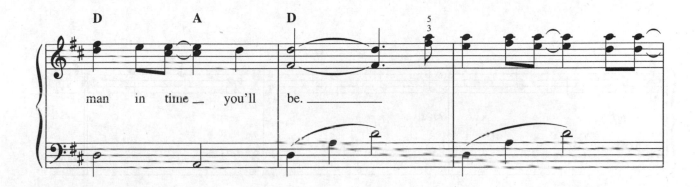

man in time_ you'll be. _____

Son of man's_ a man for all ___ to see.

SOUTHAMPTON

from the Paramount and Twentieth Century Fox Motion Picture TITANIC

By JAMES HORNER

Brightly

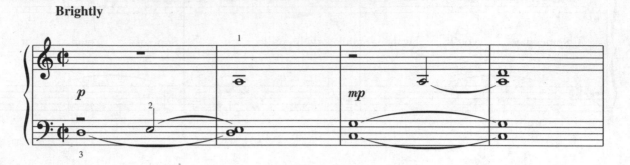

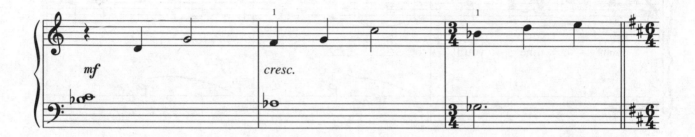

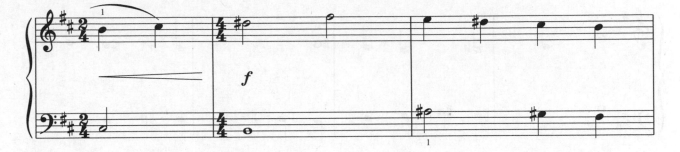

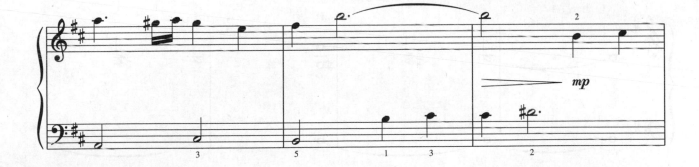

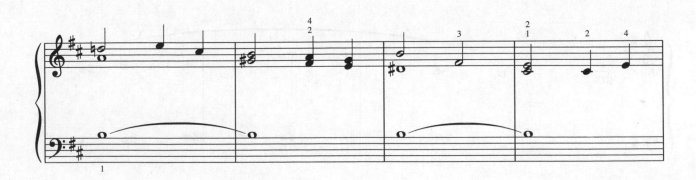

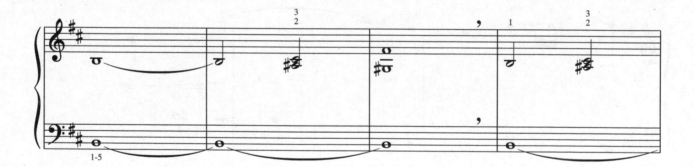

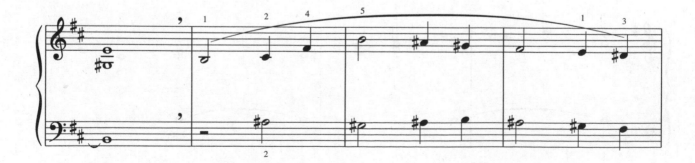

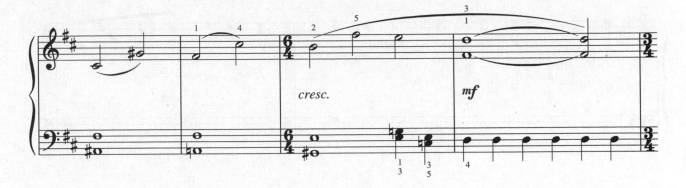

222

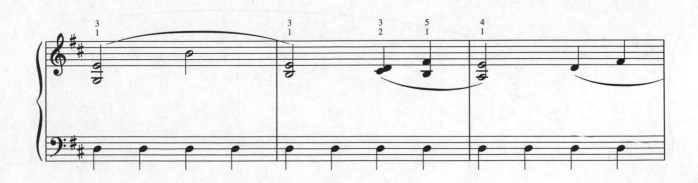

224

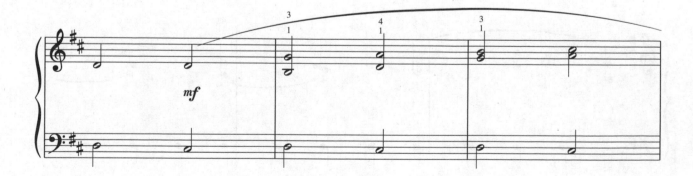

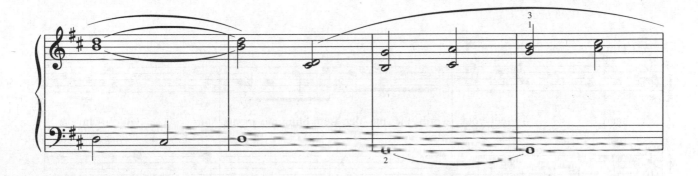

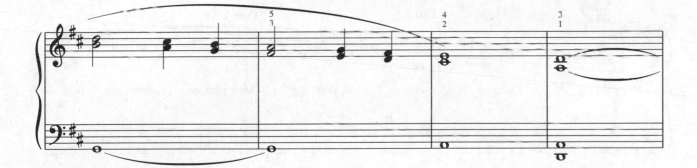

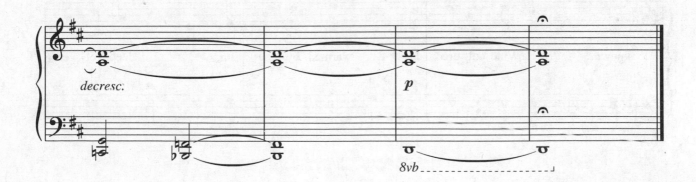

SPEAK SOFTLY, LOVE

(Love Theme)
from the Paramount Picture THE GODFATHER

Words by LARRY KUSIK
Music by NINO ROTA

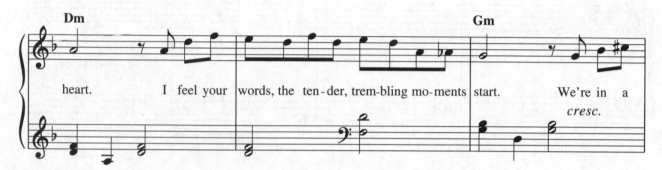

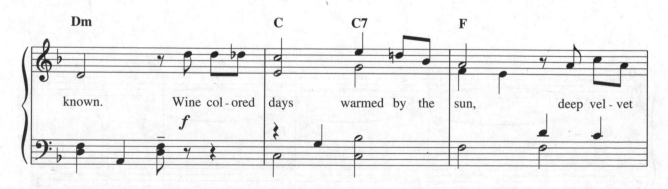

nights when we are one. Speak soft-ly, love, so no one hears us but the

sky. The vows of love we make will live un-til we

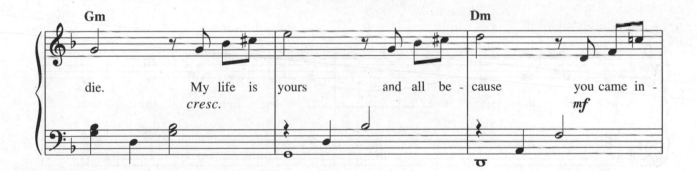

die. My life is yours and all be-cause you came in-

to my world with love so soft-ly, love. Speak soft-ly, love. love.

STRANGERS IN THE NIGHT
adapted from A MAN COULD GET KILLED

Words by CHARLES SINGLETON and EDDIE SNYDER
Music by BERT KAEMPFERT

Moderately slow

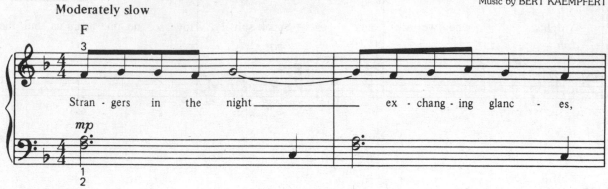

Stran - gers in the night _____ ex - chang - ing glanc - es,

won - d'ring in the night _____ what were the chanc - es

we'd be shar - ing love _____ be - fore the night was

through. _____ Some - thing in your eyes _____

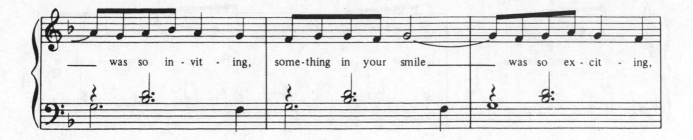

was so in-vit-ing, some-thing in your smile_____ was so ex-cit-ing,

C9   F

some-thing in my heart_____ told me I must have you._____

Am7-5

_____ Stran-gers in the night,_____ two lone-ly peo-ple we were.

D7

Stran-gers in the night_____ up to the mo-ment when we

TAKE MY BREATH AWAY
(Love Theme)
from the Paramount Picture TOP GUN

Words and Music by GIORGIO MORODER
and TOM WHITLOCK

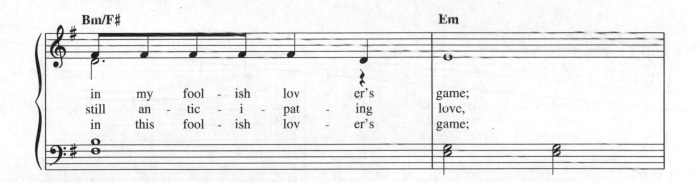

fi - n'lly lov - ers know no shame.
to be - come the fat - ed ones.
some - where there's a love in flames.

Turn - ing and re - turn - ing
Turn - ing and re - turn - ing
Turn - ing and re - turn - ing

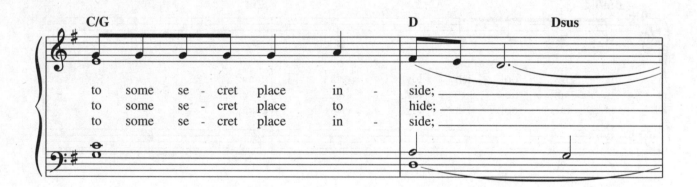

to some se - cret place in - side;
to some se - cret place to hide;
to some se - cret place in - side;

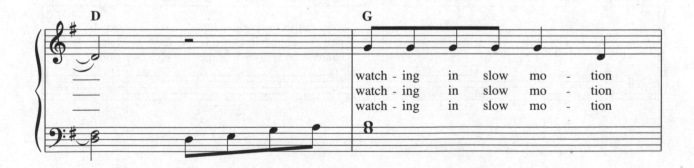

watch - ing in slow mo - tion
watch - ing in slow mo - tion
watch - ing in slow mo - tion

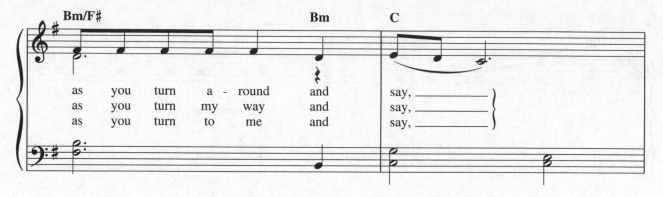

as you turn a - round and say, _____
as you turn my way and say, _____
as you turn to me and say, _____

"Take my breath a - way." _____

"Take my breath a - way." _____

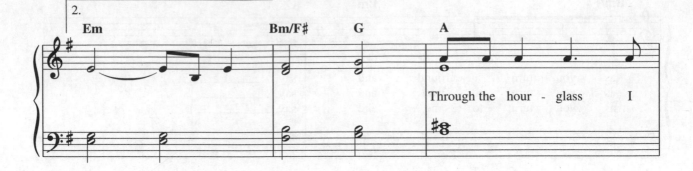

2.

Em   Bm/F#   G   A

Through the hour - glass   I

D/F#   C   G

saw you.   In time you slipped __ a - way.

A   D/F#   C

When the mirror crashed,   I called you   and   turned to hear __ you

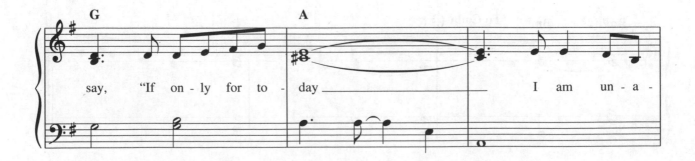

G   A

say,   "If on - ly for to - day __   I am un - a -

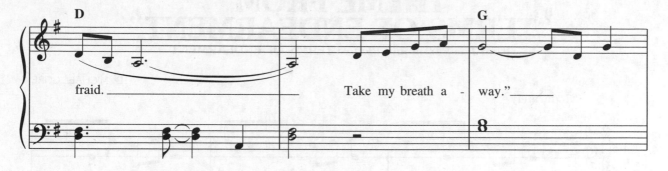

fraid. _____ Take my breath a - way." _____

D.S. al Coda

CODA

"My love, take my breath a way." _____

Repeat ad lib.

"My love, take my breath a - way."

THEME FROM
"TERMS OF ENDEARMENT"
from The Paramount Picture TERMS OF ENDEARMENT

By MICHAEL GORE

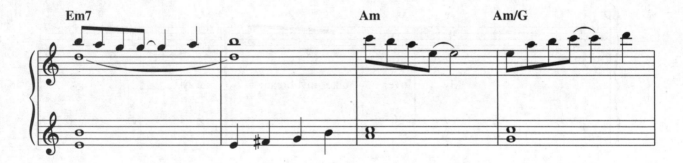

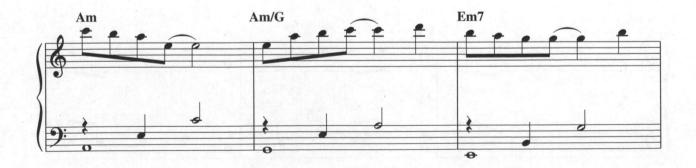

THAT'S ENTERTAINMENT
from THE BAND WAGON

Words by HOWARD DIETZ
Music by ARTHUR SCHWARTZ

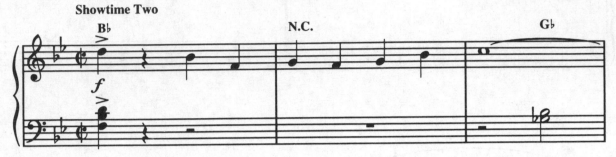

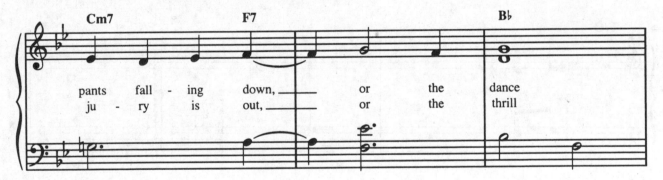

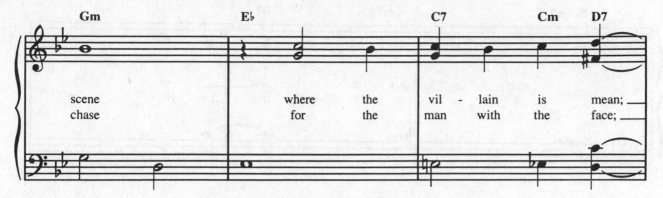

scene | | where | the | vil - lain | is | mean; ___
chase | | for | the | man | with | the | face; ___

___ | That's | en - | ter - | tain - | ment! ___
___ | That's | en - | ter - | tain - | ment! ___

___ | The | lights | | on | the
___ | The | dame | | who | is

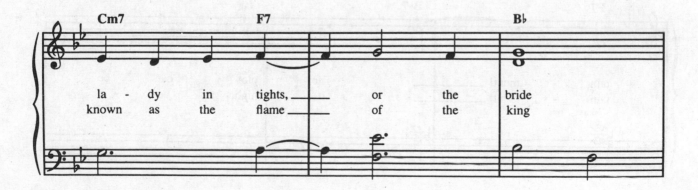

la - | dy | in | tights, ___ | or | the | bride
known | as | in the | flame ___ | of | the | king

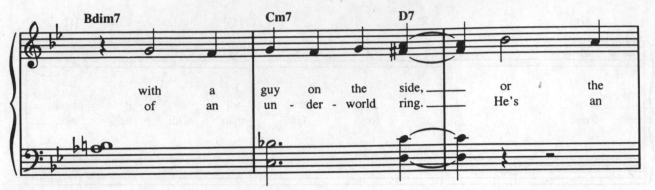

with a guy on the side,_____ or the
of an un - der - world ring._____ He's an

ball where she gives him her all;_____
ape who she won't let her es - cape;_____

That's en - ter -
That's en - ter -

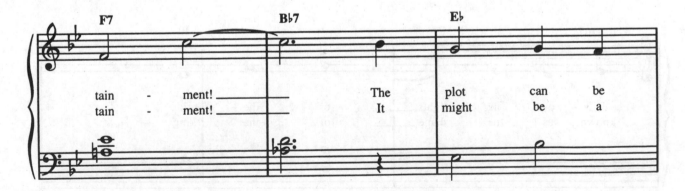

tain - ment!_____ The plot can be
tain - ment!_____ It might be a

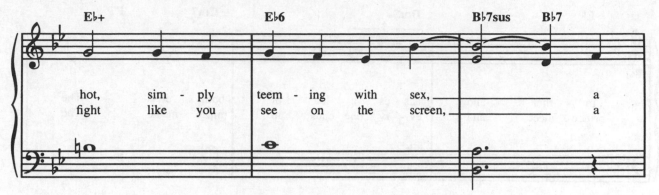

hot,   sim - ply   teem - ing   with   sex,_____   a
fight   like   you   see   on   the   screen,_____   a

gay   di - vor - cee   who   is   af - ter   her   "ex."____
swain   get - ting   slain   for   the   love   of   a   queen.____

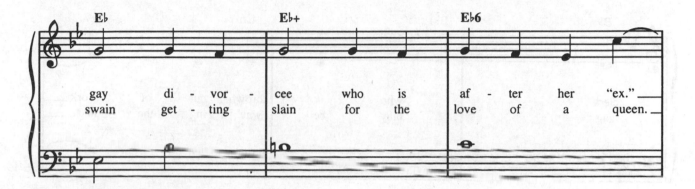

It   can   be
Some   great   Shake -

oe - di - pus   rex_____   where   a   chap   kills   his
spear - e - an   scene____   where   a   ghost   and   a

244

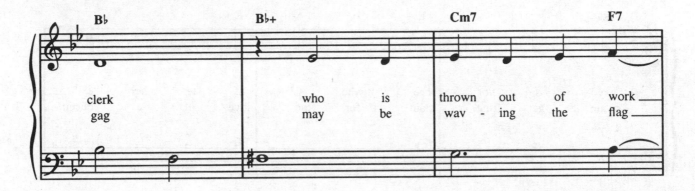

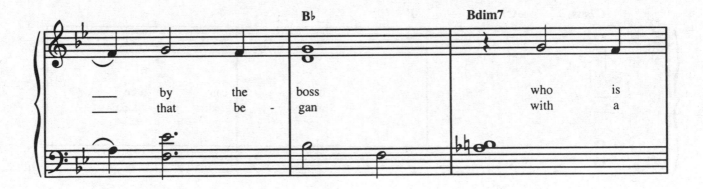

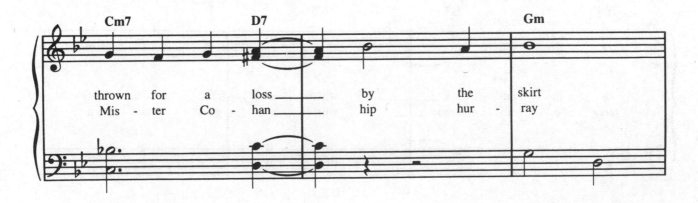

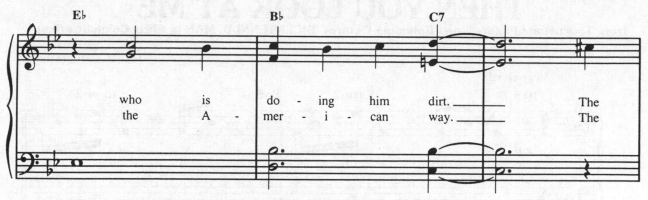

who is do - ing him dirt._____ The
the A - mer - i - can way._____ The

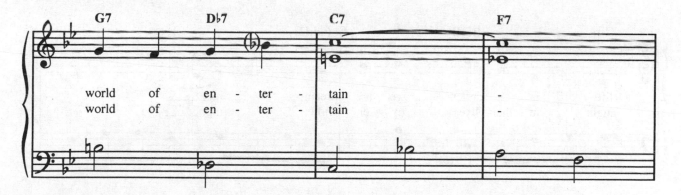

world is a stage, the stage is a
world is a stage, the stage is a

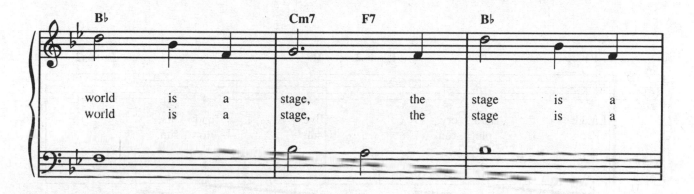

world of en - ter - tain -
world of en - ter - tain -

1.

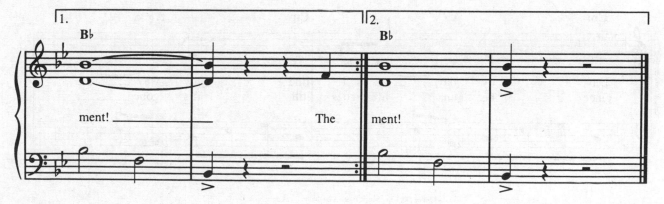

ment! _____ The
2.
ment!

THEN YOU LOOK AT ME

from Touchstone Pictures' and Columbia Pictures' BICENTENNIAL MAN (a Chris Columbus film)

Lyrics by WILL JENNINGS
Music by JAMES HORNER

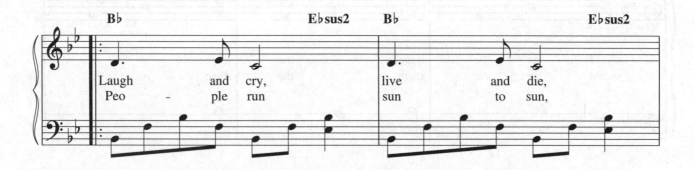

look for the soul and the mean - ing.
We have to go where it's go - ing. } Then

you look at me, __ and I al-ways see __ what I have been search - ing

for. I'm lost as can be, __ then you look at me, __ and I

am not lost an - y - more.

you look at me, ___ and I am not lost an - y -

more. And

you say you see, ___ when ___ you look at me, ___ the

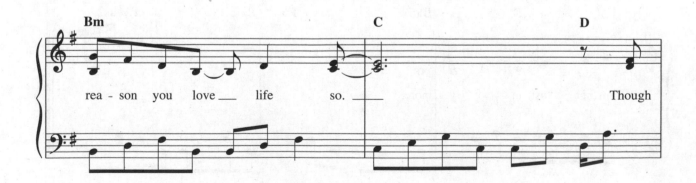

rea - son you love ___ life so. ___ Though

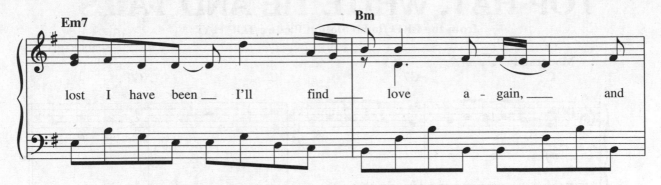

lost I have been ___ I'll find ___ love a - gain, ___ and

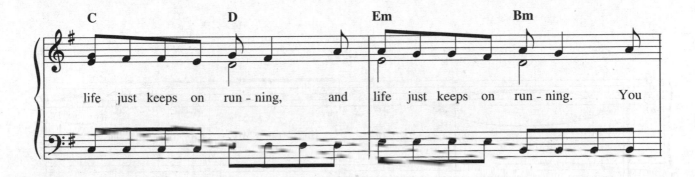

life just keeps on run - ning, and life just keeps on run - ning. You

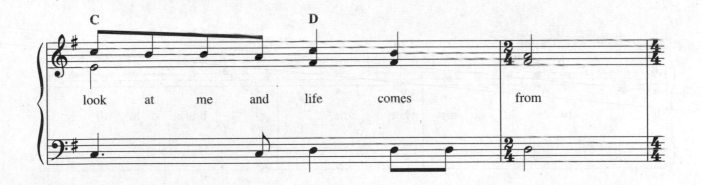

look at me and life comes from

Slower

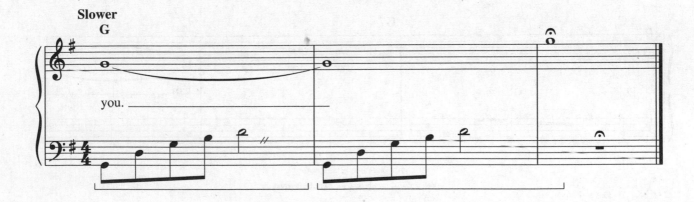

you. ___

TOP HAT, WHITE TIE AND TAILS

from the RKO Radio Motion Picture TOP HAT

Words and Music by
IRVING BERLIN

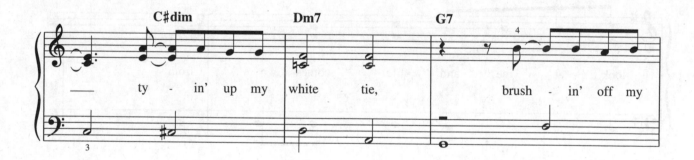

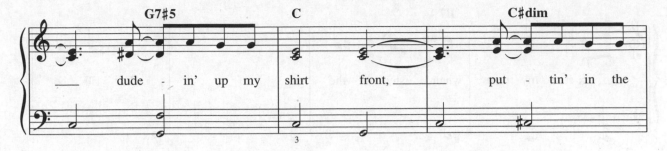

ex-cuse my dust when I step on the gas. For I'll be

there, put - tin' down my top hat,

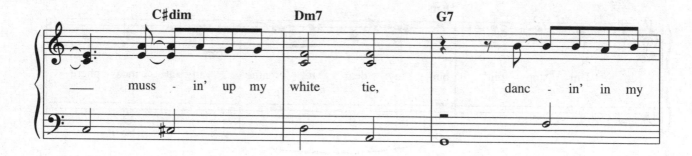

muss - in' up my white tie, danc - in' in my

tails. tails.

UNINVITED

from the Motion Picture CITY OF ANGELS

Words and Music by
ALANIS MORISSETTE

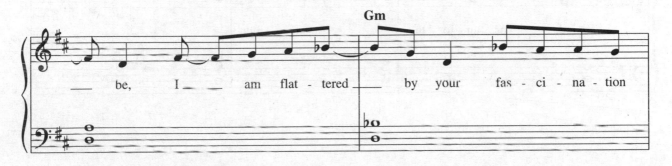

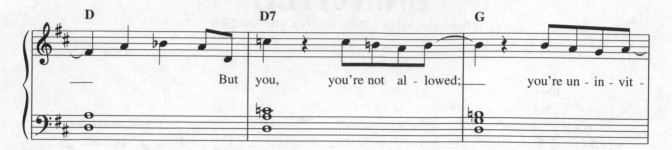

But you, you're not al - lowed; you're un - in - vit -

- ed: an un - for - tu - nate slight.

Must be strange - ly ex - cit -
Like an - y un - chart - ed ter -

- ing to watch the sto - ic squirm.
- ri - to - ry, I must seem great - ly in - trigu -

255

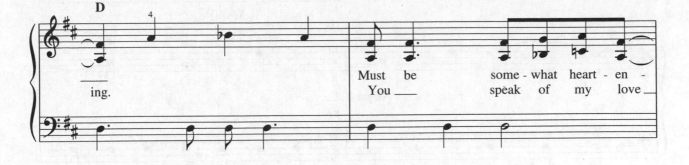

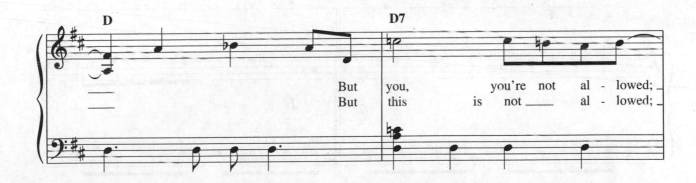

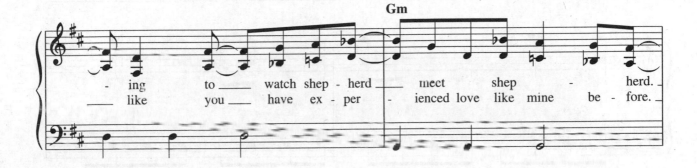

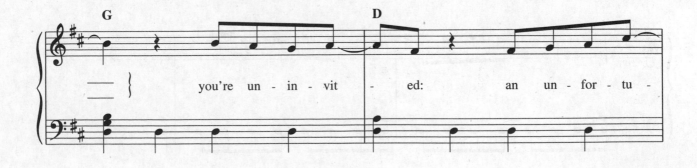

nate   slight.

I don't think you un-wor-

-thy; I need a mo - ment to de-lib-er -ate.

UP WHERE WE BELONG

from the Paramount Picture AN OFFICER AND A GENTLEMAN

Words by WILL JENNINGS
Music by BUFFY SAINTE-MARIE and JACK NITZSCHE

Slow and soulful

Who knows what to-mor-row brings; __ in a
Some hang on to "used-to-be", ___ live their

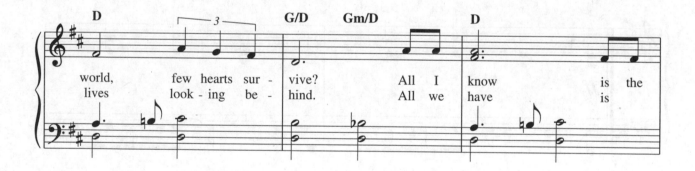

world, few hearts sur-vive? All I know is the
lives look-ing be-hind. All we have is

way I feel; __ when it's real, I keep it a-live.} The
here and now; __ all our life, out there to find.}

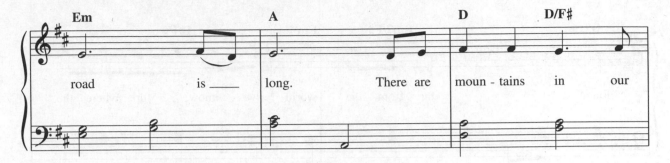

road   is _____ long.   There are   moun - tains   in   our

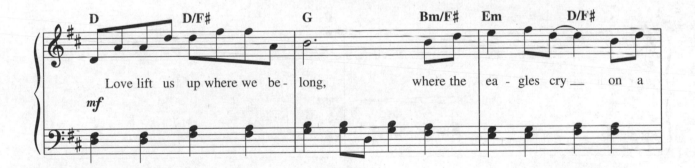

way,   but we climb   a   step ev - 'ry   day.

Love lift us up where we be - long,   where the ea - gles cry __ on a

moun - tain high.   Love lift   us   up   where we be -

long, far from the world we know, __ up where the

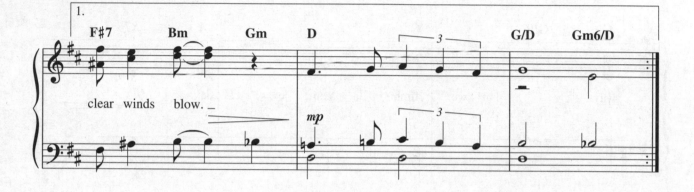

1.

clear winds blow. __

mp

2.

clear winds blow. __

mp

Time goes by, ____

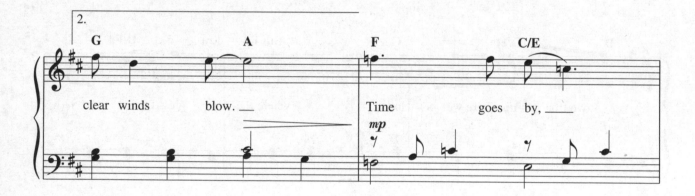

no time to cry, ____ life's you and I, ____ a-

cresc.

live to-day. _____ Love lift us up where we be-

long, where the ea-gles cry, _ on a moun-tain high.

Love lift us up where we be-long, far from the world we know, _ where the

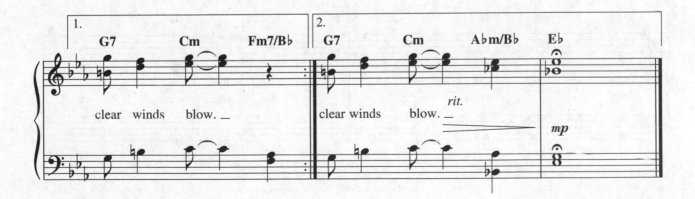

1. clear winds blow. _

2. clear winds blow. _

THE WAY WE WERE

from the Motion Picture THE WAY WE WERE

Words by ALAN and MARILYN BERGMAN
Music by MARVIN HAMLISCH

Mem - 'ries
pic - tures

light the cor - ners of my
of the smiles we left be -

mind.
hind,

Mist - y wa - ter - col - or
smiles we gave to one an -

mem - 'ries
oth - er

of the way we
for the way we

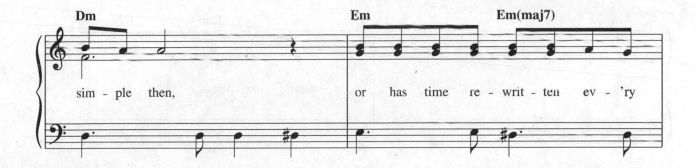

all a-gain, tell me would we?__ Could we?__

Mem - 'ries may be beau - ti - ful, and

yet, what's too pain - ful to re -

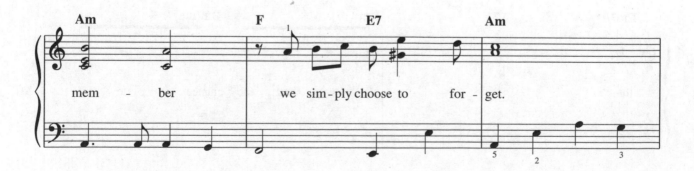

mem - ber we sim - ply choose to for - get.

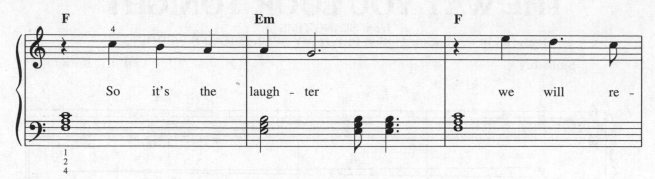

So it's the laugh - ter we will re -

mem - ber, when - ev - er we re -

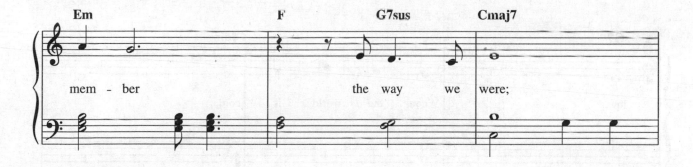

mem - ber the way we were;

the way we were. *rit.*

The Way You Look Tonight

from SWING TIME
featured in the TriStar Motion Picture MY BEST FRIEND'S WEDDING

Words by DOROTHY FIELDS
Music by JEROME KERN

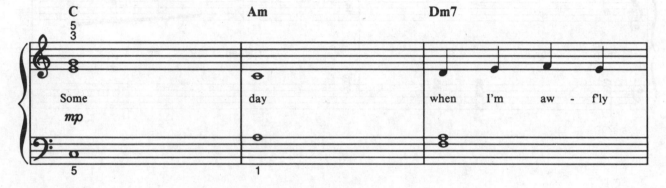

you

And the way you look to -

night.

Oh, but you're

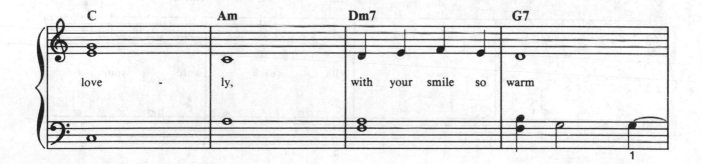

love - ly,

with your smile so warm

And your cheek so soft,

There is noth - ing

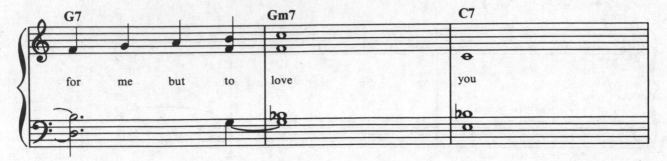

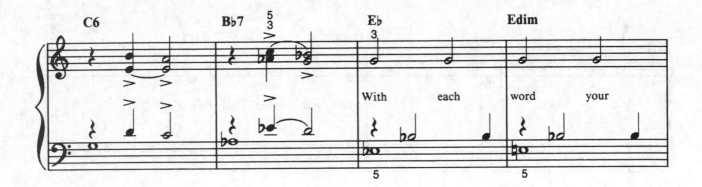

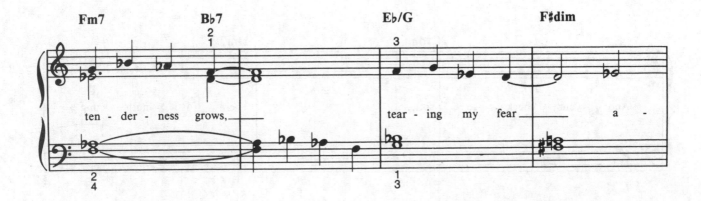

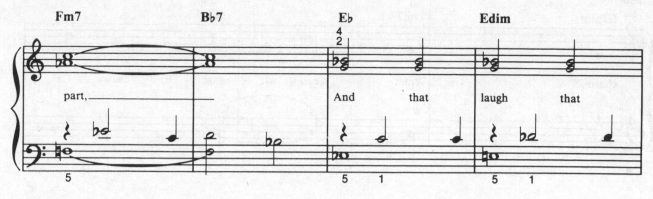

part, _____ And that laugh that

wrink - les your nose _____ touch - es my fool - ish

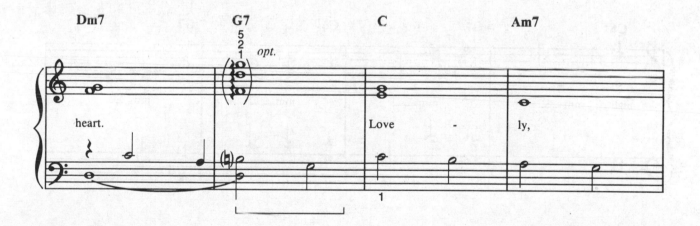

heart. Love - ly,

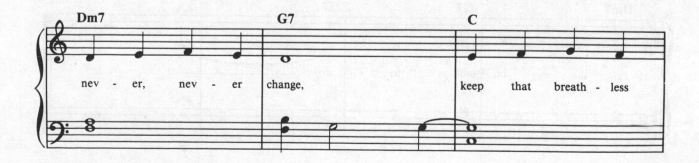

nev - er, nev - er change, keep that breath - less

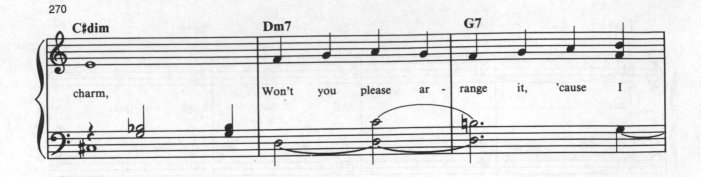

charm,   Won't you please ar - range it, 'cause I

love   you   Just   the   way   you   look   to -

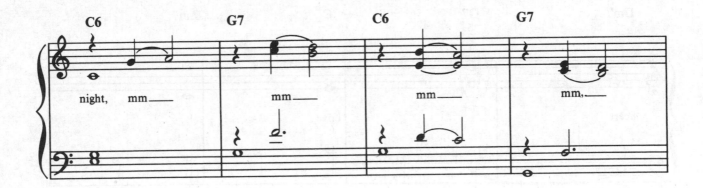

night,   mm___   mm___   mm___   mm,___

Just   the   way   you   look   to -   night.___

slower

A WINK AND A SMILE

featured in the TriStar Motion Picture SLEEPLESS IN SEATTLE

Music by MARC SHAIMAN
Lyrics by RAMSEY McLEAN

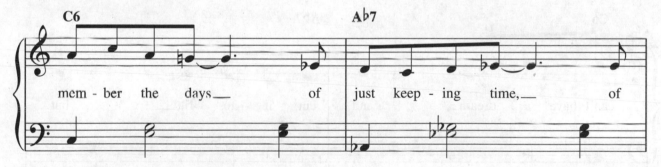

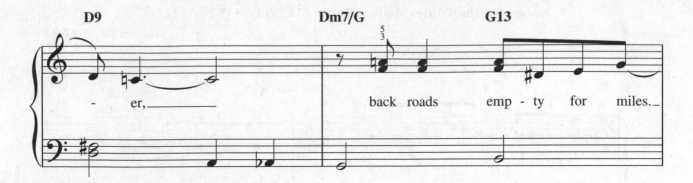

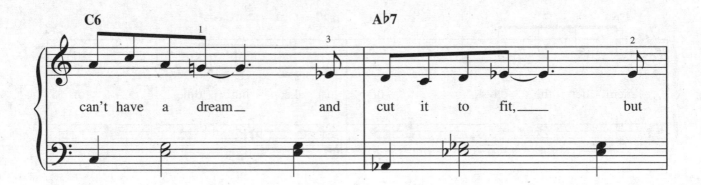

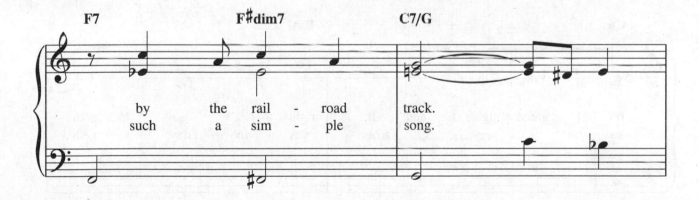

two - seat___ Cad - il - lac.___ So you can
This is where I be - long.___ Just the

rev___ her up;___ and don't___ go slow,___ it's
sound of your voice,___ the light in your eyes,___ we're

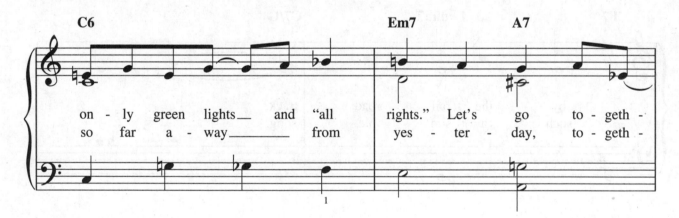

on - ly green lights___ and "all rights." Let's go to - geth -
so far a - way_____ from yes - ter - day, to - geth -

To Coda ⊕

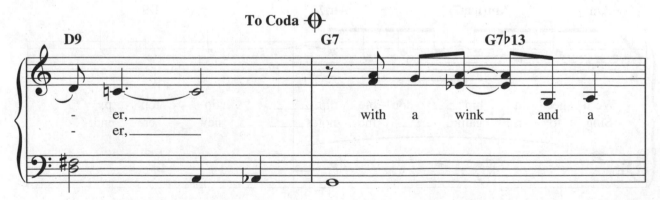

- er,_____
- er,_____ with a wink___ and a

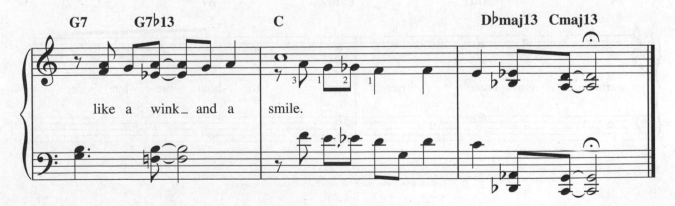

WHERE THE BOYS ARE

featured in the Motion Picture WHERE THE BOYS ARE

Words and Music by HOWARD GREENFIELD
and NEIL SEDAKA

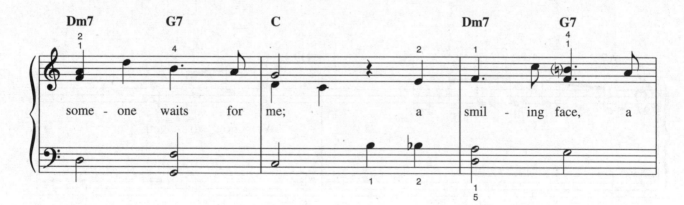

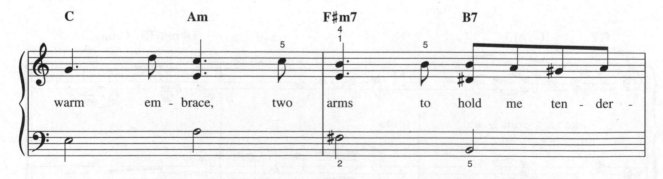

277

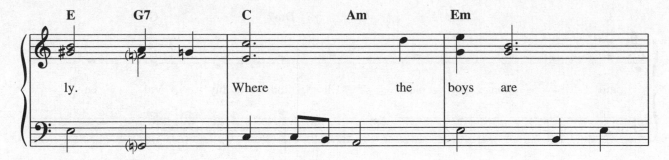

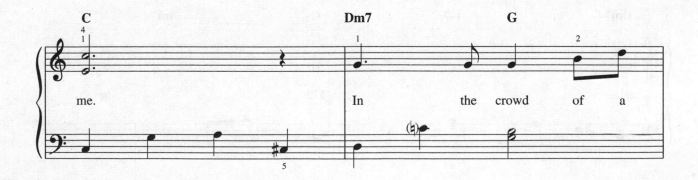

278

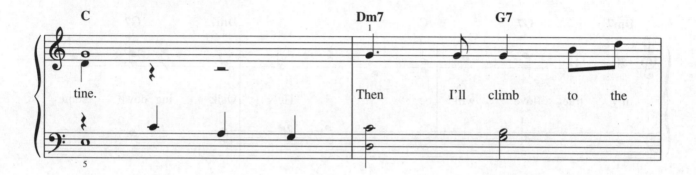

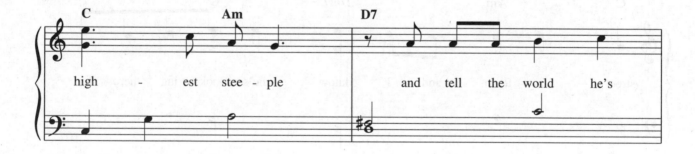

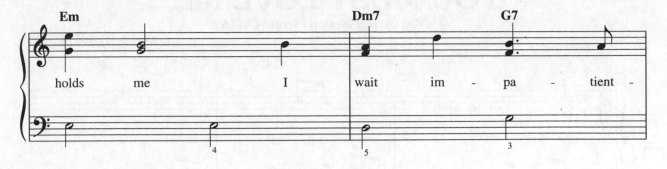

holds me I wait im - pa - tient -

ly. Where the boys are, where the

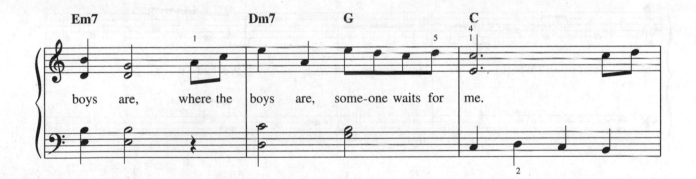

boys are, where the boys are, some-one waits for me.

YOU MUST LOVE ME

from the Cinergi Motion Picture EVITA

Words by TIM RICE
Music by ANDREW LLOYD WEBBER

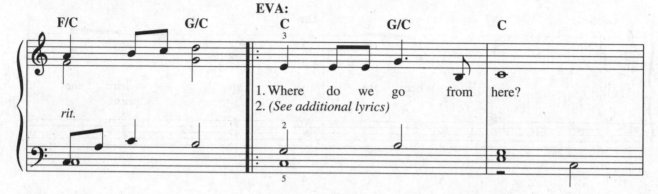

Cer-tain-ties dis-ap-pear. What do we do ___ for our

dream to sur-vive, how do we keep ___ all our pas-sions a-live as

we used to do? Deep in my heart I'm con-

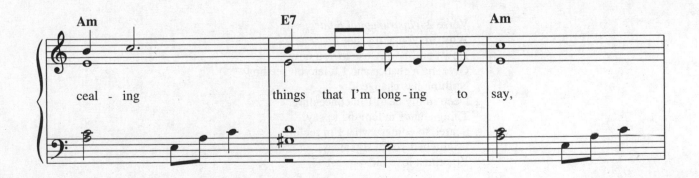

ceal-ing things that I'm long-ing to say,

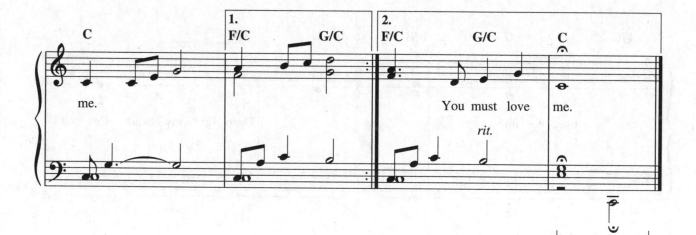

Additional Lyrics

Verse 2: *(Instrumental 8 bars)*
Why are you at my side?
How can I be any use to you now?
Give me a chance and I'll let you see how
Nothing has changed.
Deep in my heart I'm concealing
Things that I'm longing to say,
Scared to confess what I'm feeling
Frightened you'll slip away,
You must love me.

YOUR HEART WILL LEAD YOU HOME

from Walt Disney Pictures' THE TIGGER MOVIE

Words and Music by RICHARD M. SHERMAN,
ROBERT B. SHERMAN and KENNY LOGGINS

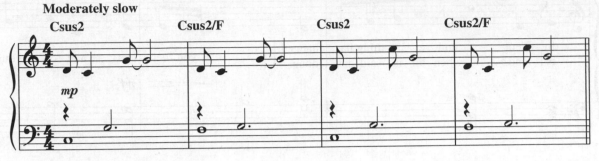

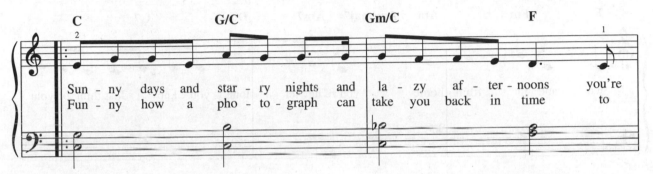

Sun - ny days and star - ry nights and la - zy af - ter - noons you're
Fun - ny how a pho - to - graph can take you back in time to

count - ing cas - tles in the clouds and hum - ming lit - tle tunes, but
plac - es and em - brac - es that you thought you'd left be - hind. They're

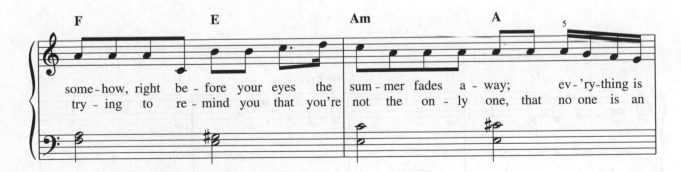

some - how, right be - fore your eyes the sum - mer fades a - way; ev - 'ry - thing is
try - ing to re - mind you that you're not the on - ly one, that no one is an

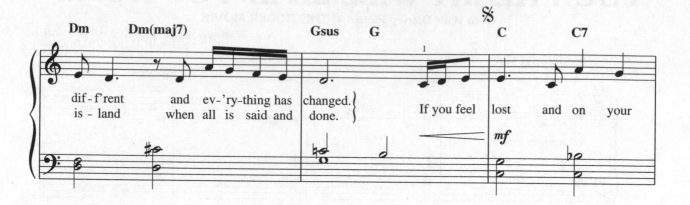

dif-f'rent and ev-'ry-thing has changed.
is-land when all is said and done.
If you feel lost and on your

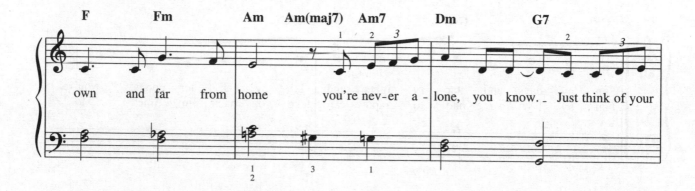

own and far from home you're nev-er a-lone, you know._ Just think of your

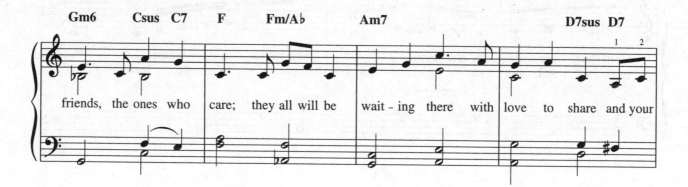

friends, the ones who care; they all will be wait-ing there with love to share and your

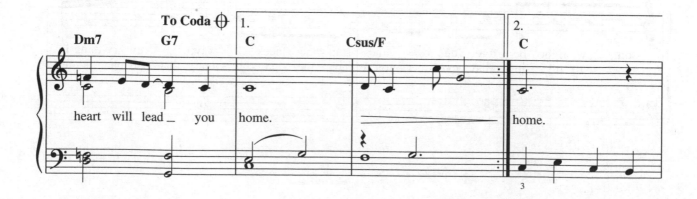

heart will lead_ you home. home.

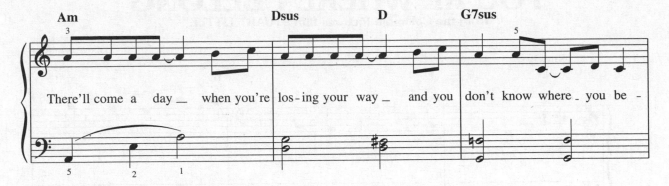

There'll come a day _ when you're los-ing your way _ and you don't know where _ you be -

long. They say that home is where the heart is, so fol-low your

heart and know that you can't go wrong. _ If you feel

home.

YOU'RE WHERE I BELONG

from the Columbia Pictures film STUART LITTLE™

Words and Music by
DIANE WARREN

I am home ___ now,
You're my first ___ taste,

home ___ now.
my first ___ taste

I've been wait - ing for ___ for -
of the sweet - est feel - ing

ev - er to find _____ you,   to find _____ you. _____
I've ev - er known, _____   that I've _____ known.

_____   I'm not a - lone _____ now, _____   a - lone _____
_____   You're my   safe _____ place, _____   my   safe

_____ now _____   'cause you've tak - en   in   my   heart from   the   cold. _____
_____ place _____   from a   world that   can   be   so   cruel and   cold. _____

_____   All   I   know is ev - 'ry   time I   look in -
_____   You're my   har - bor, you're my   shel - ter. You're that

to your eyes _____ I'm home,
wel - come smile _____ that lets me know _____

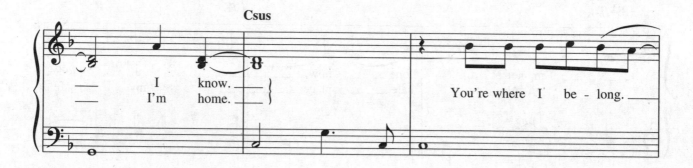

_____ I know. _____
_____ I'm home. _____
You're where I be - long. _____

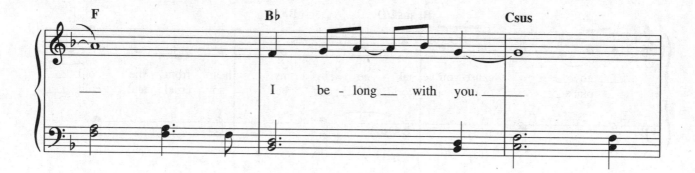

_____ I be - long _____ with you. _____

You're where I be - long _____ and I know it's the truth. _____

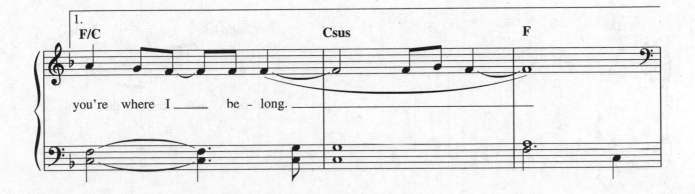

290

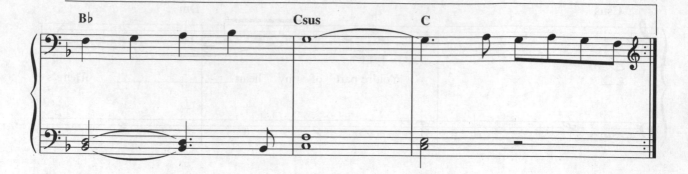

you're where I ____ be - long.

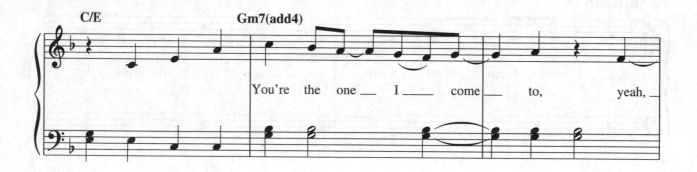

You're the one ___ I ___ come ___ to, yeah,

to keep me from ___ the cold.

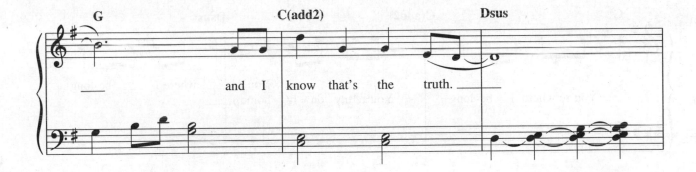

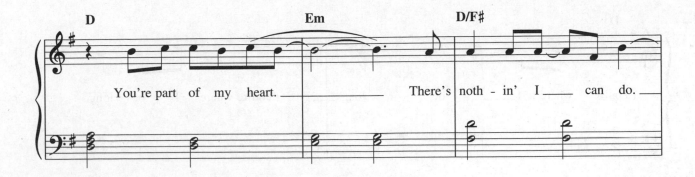

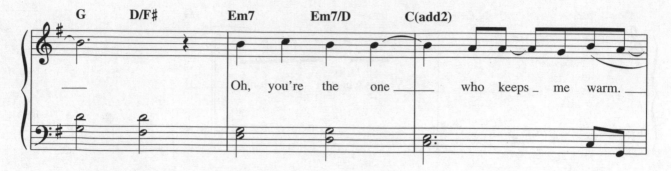

Oh, you're the one ___ who keeps _ me warm.

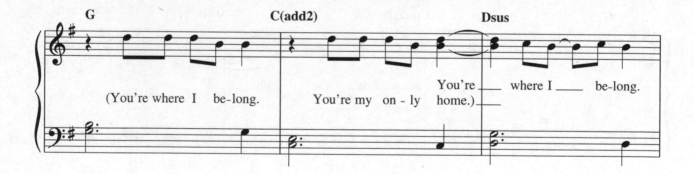

My ba - by, you're where I ___ be - long.

(You're where I be-long. You're my on - ly home.) ___ You're ___ where I ___ be-long.

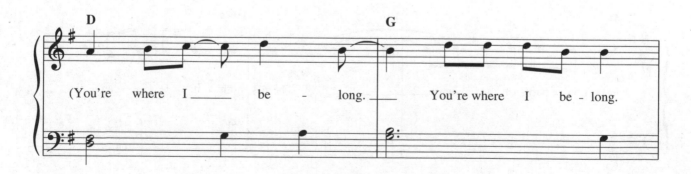

(You're where I ___ be - long. ___ You're where I be - long.

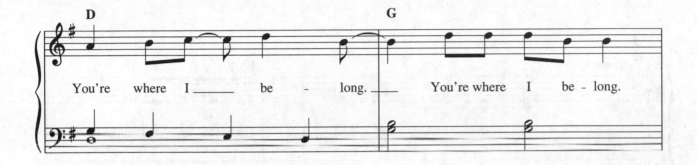

ZERO TO HERO

from Walt Disney Pictures' HERCULES

Music by ALAN MENKEN
Lyrics by DAVID ZIPPEL

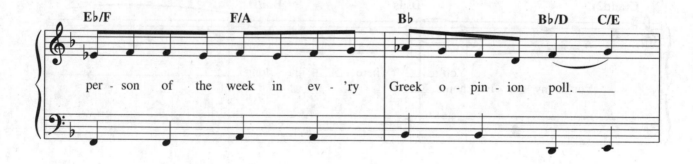

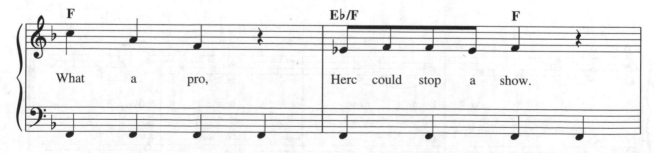

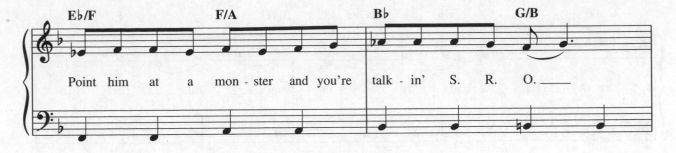

Point him at a mon-ster and you're talk-in' S. R. O. ___

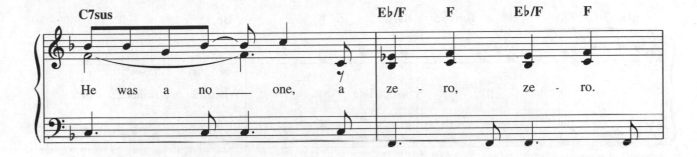

He was a no ___ one, a ze - ro, ze - ro.

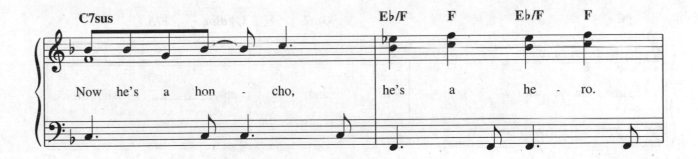

Now he's a hon - cho, he's a he - ro.

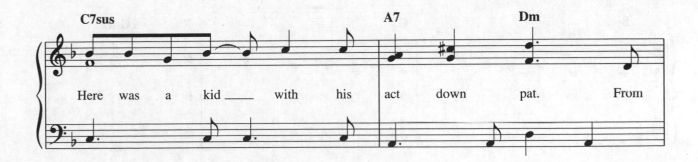

Here was a kid ___ with his act down pat. From

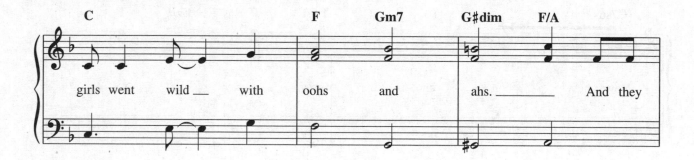

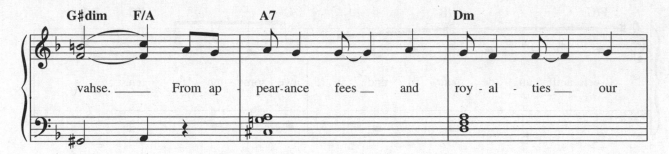

297

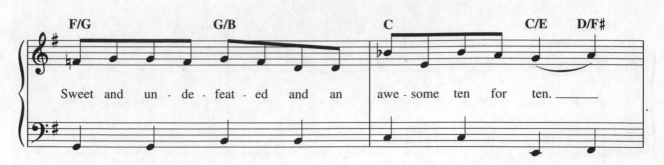

Sweet and un - de - feat - ed and an awe - some ten for ten. ____

Folks lined up just to watch him flex,

and this per - fect pack - age packed a pair of per - fect pecs.

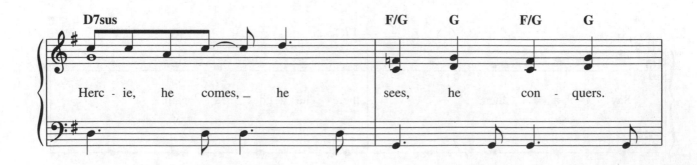

Herc - ie, he comes, __ he sees, he con - quers.

Hon - ey, the crowds _ were go - ing bon - kers.

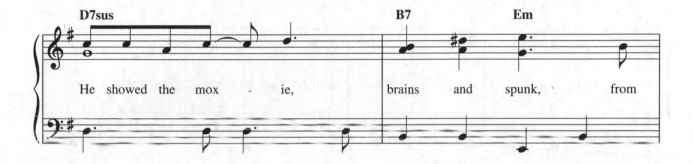

He showed the mox - ie, brains and spunk, from

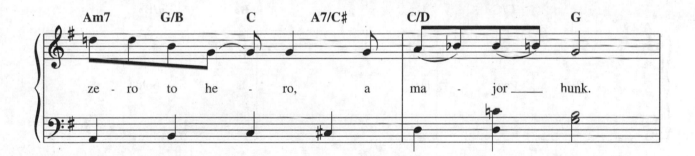

ze - ro to he - ro, a ma - jor _ hunk.

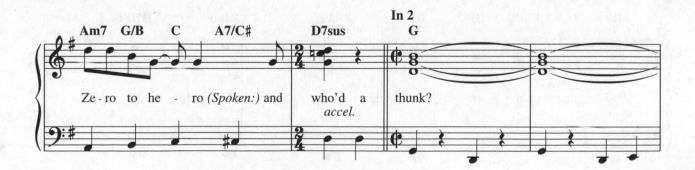

Ze - ro to he - ro *(Spoken:)* and who'd a thunk?

accel.

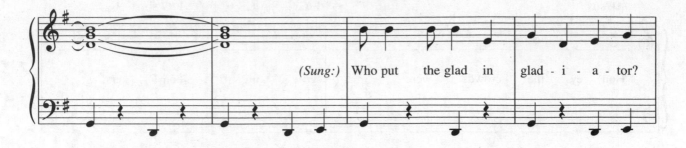

(Sung:) Who put the glad in glad - i - a - tor?

C/G   G

Her - cu - les.   Whose dar-ing deeds _ are great the - a - ter?

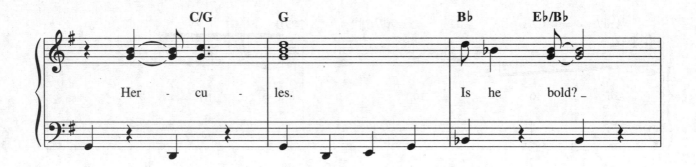

C/G   G   Bb   Eb/Bb

Her - cu - les.   Is he bold? _

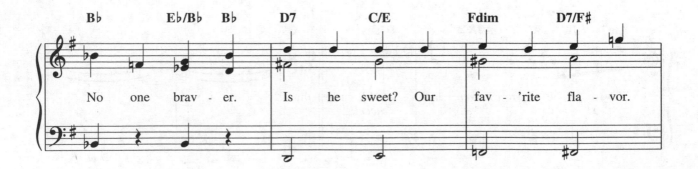

Bb   Eb/Bb Bb   D7   C/E   Fdim   D7/F#

No one brav - er. Is he sweet? Our fav - 'rite fla - vor.

Her - cu - les.   Her - cu - les.

Her - cu - les.   Her - cu - les.

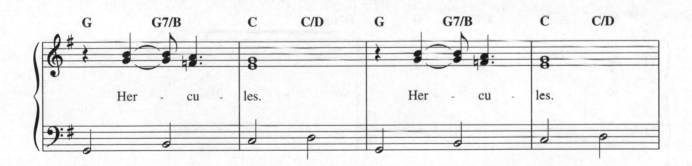

Her - cu - les.   Her - cu - les.

Bless my soul,   Herc was on a roll,   un - de -

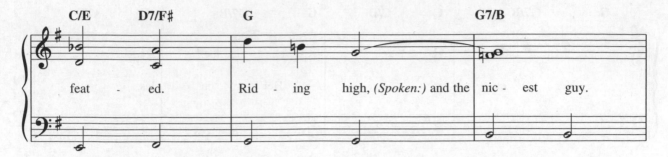

speed. From ze - ro to he - ro.

Herc is a he - ro.

Now he's a he - ro.

(Spoken:) Yes, in - deed.